The
Two Million-Year-Old Self

Number Three
CAROLYN AND ERNEST FAY SERIES
IN ANALYTICAL PSYCHOLOGY
David H. Rosen, General Editor

THE
TWO MILLION-YEAR-OLD
SELF

ANTHONY STEVENS

FOREWORD BY DAVID H. ROSEN

FROMM INTERNATIONAL PUBLISHING CORPORATION
NEW YORK

FIRST FROMM INTERNATIONAL PAPERBACK, 1997

LIBRARY OF CONGRESS CATALOGING-IN-PUBLICATION DATA

Stevens, Anthony.
    The two million-year-old self / Anthony Stevens ; foreword by
David H. Rosen
        p. cm.
    Originally published : College Station ; Texas A&M University Press,
c1993
    Includes bibliographical reference and index.
    ISBN 0-88064-214-9
    1. Archetype (Psychology) 2. Self. 3. Civilization, Modern—20th
century—Psychological aspects. 4. Dreams—Therapeutic use.
[BF175.5.A72S75   1996]
155.2—dc20

                                                    96-9215
                                                    CIP

10 9 8 7 6 5 4 3 2 1

Number Three
CAROLYN AND ERNEST FAY SERIES
IN ANALYTICAL PSYCHOLOGY
David H. Rosen, General Editor

The Carolyn and Ernest Fay edited book series, based initially
on the annual Fay Lecture Series in Analytical Psychology, was
established to further the ideas of C. G. Jung among students,
faculty, therapists, and other citizens and to enhance scholarly
activities related to analytical psychology. The Book Series and
Lecture Series address topics of importance to the individual and
to society. Both series were generously endowed by Carolyn
Grant Fay, the founding president of the C. G. Jung Educa-
tional Center in Houston, Texas. The series are in part a memo-
rial to her late husband, Ernest Bel Fay. Carolyn Fay has planted
a Jungian tree carrying both her name and that of her late husband, which will bear fruitful ideas and stimulate creative works
from this time forward. Texas A&M University and all those
who come in contact with the growing Fay Jungian tree are
extremely grateful to Carolyn Grant Fay for what she has done.
The holder of the Frank N. McMillan, Jr. Professorship in
Analytical Psychology at Texas A&M functions as the general
editor of the Fay Book Series.

Together the patient and I address ourselves to the two million-year-old man that is in all of us. In the last analysis, most of our difficulties come from losing contact with our instincts, with the age-old unforgotten wisdom stored up in us. And where do we make contact with this old man in us? In our dreams.
— C. G. Jung, *Psychological Reflections*

Two million years ago, our ancestors with brain sizes ranging from 435 cc. to 680 cc. — only a little better than the gorilla — were doing human things, cultural things. . . . They were hunting, building shelters, making tools, treating skins, living in base camps, and possibly doing many other things. . . .
— Robin Fox, *The Search for Society*

Contents

Foreword

ANTHONY STEVENS is a bridge builder. In this quintessential product from his pen, he makes connections between analytical psychology, anthropology, behavioral biology, dream psychology, psycholinguistics, psychiatry, and alternative modes of healing. Stevens once wrote to me: "Since childhood I have had a love of building bridges. Being a psychiatrist and an analyst as well as having been trained in experimental psychology, I am naturally interested in bridging the gaps between these three disciplines. In particular, I feel drawn to examine ways in which their disparate findings and theoretical constructs may parallel, complement, and ultimately fertilize one another."

Like Jung before him, Stevens meaningfully links analytical psychology with related developments in other disciplines, thus making the hypothesis of archetypes amenable to empirical study. This process began with the publication of his *Archetypes: A Natural History of the Self* in 1982, in which Stevens argued that comparative studies (mainly between ethology and analytical psychology) can throw light on the ways in which the archaic influences our lives in such fundamental areas as the development of attachment bonds; the contribution of myth, ritual, and religion to the development of personality; and the maintenance of group solidarity. In that book, he also began to associate basic Jungian concepts with structural elements of the human brain.

In his second book, *Withymead: A Jungian Community for the Healing Arts,* published in 1986, Stevens examined the primal need for community and the capacity of a group for constellating the archetype of the extended family in order to heal psychiatric illness. In his third book, *The Roots of War: A Jungian Perspective,* published in 1989, Stevens drew attention to the ease with which the primitive masculine leads us into armed conflict and killing. This volume, one of his best, also offered us ways to bring about peace.

In his fourth book, *On Jung,* which came out in 1990, he applied analytical psychology to Jung himself in a uniquely creative, biographical, and developmental treatise. In this work, he highlighted how the two million-year-old Self had helped Jung to heal his own wounds.

The Two Million-Year-Old Self is thus the product of years of excavating by Stevens in his pursuit of psychic archeology. He reveals how the archetype of the Self becomes manifest in our dreams, myths, and illnesses, and he shows us how its elemental wisdom holds the key to open the door to the therapeutic quest and the healing of our wounds.

In chapter 1, Stevens focuses on "knowing the unknowable," which is similar to exploring the "reality of the unseen" à la William James. Stevens looks at Jung's life-long objective of making the unknown known and pushing back the frontiers of the unknowable. Stevens, as a cartographer of the psyche, takes us on a journey into the mysteries of the collective unconscious where we encounter archetypes that are unknowable in themselves — in other words, not accessible to direct knowledge. Like atoms, their existence can only be inferred from their manifestations. Stevens postulates that the two million-year-old

Self lives within the dark subterranean labyrinth of the psyche. He reveals how dreams illuminate the blackness of the primeval underworld, allowing us to discover the ageless Self in this prehistoric archetypal world.

Often our egos want to know only the knowable and to dismiss the unknowable. However, as Jung experienced — and as is built into the training of all Jungian analysts — we can also know the unknowable. In order to do this, the conscious ego must surrender to a higher force, the Self (the *Imago Dei* or center and totality of the psyche); then through the experience of symbolic ego death, we can know the numinous *mysterium*. Paul Tillich arrived at this point of spiritual affirmation by having the courage to *be* in the face of nothingness. If we are patient, the light of the holy glows in the vast darkness of the seemingly chaotic collective unconscious of our inner world or psyche, which is a mirror of our outer world or universe. We can know (in the sense of gnosis) that we are a mere creative and animated spark in the never-ending process of divine evolution. How do we glimpse this?

In his second chapter, entitled Dreaming Myths, Stevens helps us open the window to our psyches and our experiences of this inner world when we dream. Stevens argues that the dream is attempting to bridge from the inside world of the psyche to the outside world. He maintains that the inner bridge builder responsible for this enormous undertaking is none other than that original genius, the two million-year-old Self. Stevens demonstrates that this supposition is in keeping with neuroscientific evidence that dreaming activity begins in the phylogenetically ancient parts of the brain. According to Stevens, "to encounter the two million-year-old within is to experience the phylogeny of our species as a personal revelation." He asks, "What could be a more amazing adventure?" Yet Stevens laments that for most of us this primordial figure, who is the constant companion of our every waking and sleeping moment, is entirely unknown.

The Talmud says, "A dream which is not interpreted is like a letter which is not read," and Stevens unravels a most interesting contemporary dream produced by Gary, a young farmer and one of his patients. He deciphers its archetypal components, showing how an ancient myth was dreamed and how it relates to Gary's situation and problem. This patient dreams a myth that allows him to transcend his neurotic conflict and proceed with his own individuation process.

People who ask "What is my personal myth and how do I live it?" have embarked on their own individuation processes to seek answers. These answers involve healing wounds as part of in-depth therapy, as suggested by Sir Francis Bacon's maxim that "wounds cannot be cured without searching." Stevens finds in his third chapter, The Healing Wound, that the search involves the two million-year-old within, who is struggling to adapt to the present world. Stevens maintains that this struggle provides us with a fundamental principle of psychopathology. He contends, "Where contemporary circumstances permit the archetypal needs of the two million-year-old to be fulfilled, the result is that form of psychic adjustment we call health, but where contemporary circumstances frustrate the archetypal needs of the two million-year-old, the result is maladjustment and illness."

To illustrate his thesis, Stevens describes the complicated psychiatric case of Jennifer. She presents with multiple psychiatric symptoms: anxiety, phobia, depression, obsessive thoughts and compulsive acts, and schizoid withdrawal. Stevens shows how all these symptoms are comprehensible as pathological exaggerations of entirely normal patterns of response for the two-million-year-old survivor. He shows how by uncovering, befriending, and casting light on the dark mysteries of this archaic inner being, Jennifer was able to overcome almost all of her obstacles. For all of us, he concludes, acceptance, empathy, bonding, and affiliation with this aboriginal Self residing in our psyches is the key to adaptation and health. In this way the so-called disturbed individual can become individuated and have a trusting and more fulfilling life.

Elisha Bartlett once wrote: "Therapeutics is not founded upon pathology. The former can not be deduced from the latter. It rests wholly upon experience. It is, absolutely and exclusively, an empirical art." In his fourth chapter, The Therapeutic Quest, Stevens considers the empirical art of healing. He looks into the success of alternative methods of treatment, such as acupuncture, chiropractic, aromatherapy, and homeopathy in the light of the two million-year-old's understanding of what it means to be ill and what is required for healing. He argues that modern medicine and psychiatry, with their emphases on science and technology, leave the two million-year-old feeling disoriented, unsupported, and misunderstood. Stevens uses data from comparative anthropology and analytical psychology to elucidate the archetype of the healer and to identify the basic principles and practices of healing that have been known to our species since the beginning of time. Stevens echoes Jung's position that the psyche represents a natural healing force. Stevens relates this to helping our inner two million-year-old Self to feel more at home in our outer contemporary world. He conjectures that we have to change our attitudes, our institutions, and our environment in order to bring the natural life of our species once more into harmony with the natural life of our planet.

This book connects a personal myth of Anthony Stevens to an archetypal myth of healing—healing ourselves and our world. It is a profound exposition, comprehensive in its breadth and inspiring in its depth. This volume is an important and timely reflection on how we must befriend the two million-year-old within and put this ancient collective wisdom into action to save ourselves, our entire human family, and our earth. We need to realize that the two million-year-old Self will continue to survive only if we survive.

I believe that in Anthony Stevens's insight lie the seeds for making the adjustment of the two million-year-old Self complete. Greater consciousness of our incarnation of the collective experience of not only humankind but other life as well would transform us and our world into a healthier state and place. Then we would truly be a united human family—harmonious and at peace with ourselves, each other, and our planet.

DAVID H. ROSEN

College Station, Texas

Acknowledgments

I WOULD LIKE TO EXPRESS MY WARMEST THANKS to Carolyn Fay and David Rosen for their kind invitation to deliver the Fay Lectures, based on a draft for this book, and for their royal hospitality while I was in Texas in April, 1992. The party that Deborah Voorhees Rosen prepared the night before my first lecture was very special, and the whole visit was, for me, life-enhancing and unforgettable.

I am immeasurably grateful to "Gary" and "Jennifer" for permitting me to tell the most significant parts of their histories. The privilege of working with such patients has made my life worth living and this book possible.

I must thank Routledge and Princeton University Press for permission to quote from *The Collected Works of C. G. Jung*, Routledge, William Collins, and Random House for permission to quote from *Memories, Dreams, Reflections* by C. G. Jung, recorded and edited by Aniela Jaffé, and the University of Toronto Press for allowing me to use Dr. P. D. MacLean's famous diagram of the triune brain.

My special thanks go to Norma Luscombe for her unfailing care, diligence, and good humor in word processing my original manuscript and to Mary Lenn Dixon for her zeal in editing the finished product.

The
Two Million-Year-Old Self

Prologue

AT THE HEART OF JUNGIAN PSYCHOLOGY is the idea that beneath
our conscious intelligence a deeper intelligence is at work — the
evolved intelligence of humankind. By personifying this phylogenetic component of the psyche as an archaic being, or "the
two million-year-old man that is in us all," Jung lay himself
at the mercy of any beady logician wishing to accuse him of
falling into a homuncular fallacy — namely, that he believed he
had a little old man in there sitting at the controls. But Jung
labored under no such delusion. To him, the two million-year-
old was a vivid metaphor for an age-old dynamic at the core
of personal existence, there by virtue of the evolutionary heritage of our species. He applied it in the same spirit as Neils
Bohr, who referred to the atom as a "miniature solar system":
both are valid attempts to create a working image of what cannot otherwise be seen.

Jung discovered that the archetypal units of which the phylogenetic (biologically evolved) psyche is composed *personate* in
dreams and fantasies. We do not encounter masculinity, femi-
ninity, evil, or wisdom as intellectual abstractions, but as hu-

man figures with personalities and intentions of their own. When Jung met them in his patients and in himself, he named them the animus, the anima, the shadow, and the wise old man and woman. The two million-year-old was another such personification: this archaic presence does not have a physical existence inside our heads, any more than the "soul" or the "unconscious," but as the phenomenological embodiment of our evolutionary inheritance, it can be understood as playing an indispensable role in the drama of our personal lives, "personating" as a companion whom it is possible, as I have learned, to recognize, cherish, and befriend.

A strength of Jungian psychology (also a grave danger) is its love of the esoteric, its willingness to go its own way. Unfortunately, this self-reliant intrepidity can lead to the kind of psychic parochialism for which James Hillman is so staunch an advocate. In his fascinatingly provocative book *The Dream and the Underworld* he proclaims, "The tradition of depth psychology is to stay at home and create its own ground as it proceeds." This is treacherous ground on which to build a psychology: vaporous ground, ground fit only for building castles in the air. Wishing to sustain this somewhat agoraphobic tradition, Hillman asserts that Freud and Jung both "abjured anatomy, biology, natural science, and theology for their basic premises."[1] But this is not entirely true; certainly not of the first three disciplines named. Freud elected to stay at home faute de mieux because neurophysiology was not sufficiently advanced for him to develop his "Project for a Scientific Psychology" as he originally intended. As it was, his psychoanalytic formulations were profoundly influenced by the neurophysiological knowledge he acquired working for six formative years in the laboratory of the great Ernst Brücke. Jung, like Freud, acknowledged the fundamental importance of "the 'psychic infra-red', the biological instinctual pole of the psyche," which "gradually passes over into the physiology of the organism and thus merges with its chemical and physical conditions."[2] This biological pole of the archetype Jung compared to the ethological "pattern of behaviour" and declared it to be "the proper concern of scientific psychology."[3]

Rather than stay at home, I would have us journey far into the past and way over the horizon into cultures remote from the traditions of Western psychology. And rather than restrict ourselves to historical parallels from the relatively recent Sumerian, Egyptian, Greek, or Roman past, I would go back much further, back to the hunter-gatherer existence for which our psyches were formed, back to the archetypal foundations of all human experience, back to the hominid, mammalian, and reptilian ancestors who live on in the structures of our minds and brains. To do this is to discover within Jung's two million-year-old person, a 140 million-year-old vertebrate, which supports our finite existence and animates our dreams.

I.

Knowing the Unknowable

*We must constantly bear in mind that what we mean by "archetype"
is in itself irrepresentable, but has effects which make visualizations
of it possible, namely, the archetypal images and ideas. We meet
with a similar situation in physics: there the smallest particles are
themselves irrepresentable but have effects from the nature of which
we can build up a model.*
—C. G. JUNG, *Collected Works*, vol. 8

A PASSIONATE URGE TOWARDS UNDERSTANDING

AS EDUCATED MEMBERS OF WESTERN SOCIETY, we share a number
of common assumptions: one of these is that we are potentially
capable of knowing everything that is knowable. We are shaken
out of this illusion only when we begin to push knowledge
to its limits and ask such questions as what is "knowledge"
and how can we "know" anything? What existed before the
universe came into being? What is the essence of all creation?
Why does anything exist at all? When we pose questions like
this, the possibility begins to dawn on us that there may be
things that lie beyond our capacity to grasp, know, or even
imagine, let alone understand.

Yet these are the sort of questions that intrigue children.
Just as all children are natural artists, so they are also natural
metaphysicians. The naive questions they ask often possess a pro-

fundity that a lifetime of dedicated research could not fathom. Why is the earth? Where did God come from? What is death? Why do we have to die? What makes us live? Mommy, where was I before Daddy put me in your tummy? When I asked my mother that question at the age of five, her shocking answer— "I don't know darling"—sent me off on my first experience of active imagination: I had spent eternity waiting on a cloud, waiting for the summons to my parents' bedchamber—it was extremely boring. That experience taught me how miraculously fortunate I am to be here, how precious life is, how one must cherish it and savor every day as it passes.

Their preoccupation with origins makes children mythologically and epistemologically inclined. Most of them lose this inclination because most adults in our society do not share it. However, a few never cease the epistemological quest. They are the ones who go on to become scientists, philosophers, psychologists. They are driven to find answers to naive questions. When they find them, the answers only give rise to more questions, and they are hooked for life on their own speciality. One such was Jung.

When, at eighty-two, he began his autobiography with the words "My life is a story of the self-realization of the unconscious," it is significant that he wrote *the* unconscious, not *my* unconscious, for what fascinated him was the universal human unknown that, generation after generation, seeks incarnation in the world. Looking back on his life, he wrote: "In my case it must have been a passionate urge towards understanding which brought about my birth. For that is the strongest element in my nature."[1] He accepted that we are all born with "a need to know," but he felt he had been endowed with a special gift in that direction.

This special gift enabled him to perceive the archetypal patterns at work behind typical events. The fact, which he frequently acknowledged, that archetypes are transcendent, irrepresentable, and therefore unknowable in themselves, merely enhanced their fascination for him.

Jung's epistemological mission—his need to know—gave him a lasting affinity with the Gnostics. The early Christian sect of gnosticism (Greek *gnostikos,* one who knows) held that *gnosis* (knowledge), must be distinguished from *sophia* (wisdom) and *epistēmē* (general knowledge), since gnosis differs from other kinds of knowledge: it is derived not from ordinary sources or via the senses but directly from God through special revelation. Jung believed that he had received such a revelation in his adolescent vision of God defecating on the roof of Basel Cathedral. And it made him intolerant of his father's timidity in confronting his own loss of faith. Whenever Jung tackled him, his father became irritable and defensive: "You always want to *think,*" he would complain. "One ought not to think, but *believe.*" Jung couldn't stand this: "No," he thought, "one must *experience* and *know!*" These encounters with his spiritually bankrupt father confirmed Jung in his gnosticism—as one dedicated to knowing and experiencing the reality of the psyche.[2]

It also went along with a need to test and to question. Although deeply attracted to Freud, who was in all important respects his father's opposite, Jung could never accept Freud's formulations of the basic concepts of psychoanalysis as ex cathedra statements of established wisdom. He had to test them, first with the word association test, then later through his observation of schizophrenics and his studies in mythology. Despite Freud's extreme displeasure, he questioned two of the fundamental hypotheses of psychoanalysis, namely, (1) that libido is exclusively sexual (Jung didn't think it was) and (2) that the unconscious is entirely personal and peculiar to the individual (Jung came to see that it was much more than that and that all human beings share a common psychic structure).

Jung's discovery that schizophrenic delusions had mythic parallels was for him an intellectual watershed. It convinced him that Freud's view was so narrowly personalistic that it blinded him to the existence of the suprapersonal psyche shared by us all by virtue of our humanity. Jung called it the natural mind, a dynamic and universal substratum on which our private world is built. To define and establish this basis on which personal awareness grows was the task that absorbed the rest of his life, and his hypotheses of the archetype and the collective unconscious were the "guiding fictions" (to use Adler's phrase) that, after his break with Freud, enabled him to proceed on his way.

When Jung stated that the archetypes—the fundamental units of the natural mind—were essentially unknowable, what exactly did he mean? He meant that they were not accessible to *direct* knowledge. For Jung, *private* experience, *inner* knowledge, *gnosis* were primary. All else was inferential, in that the existence of an archetype could only be inferred from its manifestations in myths, psychotic delusions, and dreams, especially "big" dreams, or "culture pattern dreams" as the anthropologists call them.

Jung's own "experiment with the unconscious," conducted between 1914 and 1918 in neutral Switzerland, was later validated and interpreted in the light of his expeditions to the Elgonyi in East Africa and the Indians of New Mexico. These researches confirmed for him the validity of three crucial hypotheses: (1) that the psyche is the primary datum—not only of psychology but of our lives; (2) that it is objective inasmuch as we do not construct our psyche or will it into being: it exists a priori, a product of nature, or evolution; and (3) that the basic unit of the objective psyche is the archetype—the archetype of the collective unconscious. It choreographs the basic patterns we dance to throughout life. It is the archetype, not our con-

scious ego, that pays the fiddler and calls the tune, as Matthew
Arnold understood:

> Born into life—we bring
> A bias with us here,
> And, when here, each new thing
> Affects us we come near;
> To tunes we did not call our being must keep chime.
> —*Empedocles on Etna*, 1852

THE ARCHETYPES OF THE COLLECTIVE UNCONSCIOUS

As the basic concept of Jungian psychology, the archetype is
of comparable significance to gravity in Newtonian physics, rela-
tivity in Einsteinian physics, or natural selection in Darwinian
biology. It is psychology's quantum theory: one of the most
important ideas to emerge in the twentieth century, possessing
far-reaching implications for both the social and the natural
sciences—though practitioners of these sciences have been slow
to acknowledge the fact. As we shall see, they are beginning
to catch up.

As Heraclitus justly observed, "The real constitution of each
thing is accustomed to hide itself." Just as the physicist investi-
gates particles and waves and the biologist genes, so it is the
province of the psychologist to investigate archetypes: for archetypes are the functional units of which the collective unconscious is composed, and together they make up "the archaic
heritage of humanity." Jung described them as "a living system
of reactions and aptitudes that determine the individual's life
in invisible ways."[3]

The problem with this formulation was that it savored too
much of Darwinism for social scientists and the academic es-
tablishment to accept. As a result, Jung's announcement of his

theory of archetypes was never granted the attentive recognition it deserved. Why should this be?

To understand the reasons for this neglect, we must turn briefly to the history of ideas since Darwin's time. Unfortunately, the early sociologists embraced Darwin too eagerly, misapplying such concepts as the struggle for existence and survival of the fittest to political phenomena, thus giving rise to the disreputable movement known as Social Darwinism. There is no doubt that Social Darwinism was put to evil use. Imperialists used it to justify the extermination of primitive populations, Marxists used it to incite massacre in the service of the class struggle, Hitler used it to fuel his fantasies of world domination and to justify his genocide of the Slavs and the Jews, criminologists used it as an argument in favor of capital punishment and castration, eugenicists used it as a justification of selective euthanasia, and militarists used it everywhere as a justification for war.

With this catalog of crimes to its discredit, it is not hard to understand why there should have been a revulsion against all aspects of Social Darwinism and that it should result in a rejection of biological concepts in the study of human psychology. So the pendulum swung hard in the opposite direction and the "innate" became a taboo subject in university departments throughout the world. Liberalism meant environmentalism, behaviorism, and the apotheosis of the tabula rasa—the blank slate on which life, through some disembodied miracle, contrived to inscribe all its lessons without any assistance from the evolutionary past.

As the pendulum swung, so the clock turned back—back to that pre-Darwinian empiricism so beloved of our Anglo-Saxon intellectual tradition: the notion that all concepts are derived from experience and that the "innate" plays no part in the matter whatever. How does the human mind come "to be furnished with that vast store which the busy and boundless fancy of man has painted on it?" asked John Locke, the arch-empiricist, who answered himself, "in one word, from *experience*."[4]

In this climate, Jung was unlikely to get a fair hearing, nor did he. It was in vain for him to protest that he was not arguing for innate ideas. Archetypes, he said, are not inherited *ideas* but inherited *possibilities* of ideas—a statement any biologist would find acceptable, but, until recently, no psychologist. Instead of receiving a sympathetic hearing, Jung was accused of being a fascist, an anti-Semite, and a Nazi sympathizer, while the behaviorists, with a clear conscience and in the service of liberal democracy, continued to develop their "laws of learning," apparently unaware that every tyrant in the world had promptly misappropriated these very laws so as to torture, brainwash, and intimidate their hapless subjects. "Of course Behaviourism works!" snorted W. H. Auden. "So does torture. Give me a no-nonsense, down-to-earth behaviourist, a few drugs and simple electrical appliances, and in six months I will have him reciting the Athanasian Creed in public."[5]

Though few seemed to realize it, Jung's hypothesis of the archetype in fact transcended the nature-versus-nurture debate and healed the Cartesian split between body and mind. He proposed not only that the archetypal structures were fundamental to the existence and survival of all living organisms but that they were continuous with structures controlling the behavior of inorganic matter as well. The archetype was no mere psychic entity but "the bridge to matter in general." It was this "psychoid" aspect of the archetype that was taken up by the physicist Wolfgang Pauli, who believed it made a major contribution to our ability to comprehend the principles on which the universe had been created.[6]

Since archetypes precondition all existence, they are manifest in the spiritual achievements of art, science, and religion, as well as in the organization of organic and inorganic matter. The archetype thus provides a basis for a common understanding of data derived from all sciences and all human activities — not least because of its implications for epistemology, the study of knowledge per se.

ARCHETYPAL MANIFESTATIONS

Since archetypes-as-such are unknowable, their existence can only be inferred from their manifestations. The manifestations of primary interest to psychologists are those typically human attributes which the archetypes give rise to in the course of the life cycle — the parallel thoughts, images, mythologems, feelings, and patterns of behavior that occur in people everywhere, irrespective of their class, creed, race, geographical location, or historical time.

"Although the changing situations of life must appear infinitely various to our way of thinking," wrote Jung, "their possible number never exceeds certain natural limits; they fall into more or less typical patterns that repeat themselves over and over again. The archetypal structure of the unconscious *corresponds to the average run of events*. The changes that may befall a man are not infinitely variable; they are variations of certain typical occurrences which are limited in number. When therefore a distressing situation arises, the corresponding archetype will be constellated in the unconscious. Since this archetype is *numinous,* i.e., possesses a specific energy, it will attract to itself the contents of consciousness — conscious ideas that render it perceptible and hence capable of conscious realization."[7]

Just how indispensable the archetypal concept is in practice can be judged from the manner in which researchers in many other disciplines keep rediscovering the hypothesis and reannouncing it in their own terminology. So numerous are the instances of this, that it is possible to examine only a fraction of them here. I will confine myself to examples of archetypal functioning that are to be found in anthropology, behavioral biology, dream psychology, psychiatry, and psycholinguistics.

ANTHROPOLOGY: CULTURAL UNIVERSALS AND THE ARCHETYPAL SOCIETY

There is a principle that I believe should be elevated to the status of a fundamental law of anthropology, and I am glad to say that shortly before his death I was able to persuade the great anthropologist Victor Turner of the validity of this law.[8] It can be stated as follows: whenever a phenomenon is found to be characteristic of all human communities, irrespective of culture, race, or historical epoch, then it is an expression of an archetype of the collective unconscious.

The fact of the matter is that all cultures, whatever their geographical location or historical era, display a large number of social characteristics which are in themselves absolutely diagnostic of a specifically human culture. These have been cataloged independently by George Murdock and Robin Fox. According to these anthropologists, no human culture is known that lacks laws about property, procedures for settling disputes, rules governing courtship, marriage, and adultery, taboos relating to food and incest, rules of etiquette prescribing forms of greeting and modes of address, the manufacture of tools and weapons, cooperative labor, visiting, feasting, hospitality, gift-giving, the performance of funeral rites, belief in the supernatural, religious rituals, the recital of myths and legends, dancing, mental illness, faith healing, dream interpretation, and so on.[9]

All such universal patterns of behavior are evidence of archetypes at work. The point is that what any one of us experiences in life is not determined merely by our personal histories.

It is also fundamentally guided by the collective history of the human species as a whole. This collective history is biologically encoded in the collective unconscious, and the code owes its origins to a past so remote as to be shrouded in the primordial mists of evolutionary time.

The archetypal endowment, with which each of us is born, guides and controls the life cycle of our species — birth and being mothered, exploring the environment, showing wariness of strangers, playing in the peer group, being initiated as an adult member of the community, establishing a place in the social hierarchy, bonding between males for hunting and out-group hostilities, courting, marrying, child-rearing, participating in religious rituals, assuming the social responsibilities of advanced maturity, and the preparation for death. Jung summed it all up in a memorable aphorism: "Ultimately, every individual life is at the same time the eternal life of the species."[10]

The cross-cultural evidence is fascinating and overwhelming in its implications. But for most of this century, anthropologists have displayed little interest in cultural universals, preferring to stress the differences between cultures and relating these differences not to biological factors but to child-rearing practices and geographical, climatic, and economic characteristics. This again is an example of academic prejudice in favor of environmentalism and in hostility to evolutionary biology. However, there have been notable exceptions. During the years when Jung was growing up in Klein Hüningen and later attending the university in Basel, a German ethnologist named Adolf Bastian was traveling all over the world studying the myths, folklore, and customs of widely differing peoples. What greatly impressed Bastian was the similarity he noted between the themes and motifs he encountered wherever he went. He noticed, however, that these universal themes, which he called *Elementargedanken* (elementary ideas), invariably manifested themselves in local forms, peculiar to the group of people he happened to be studying at the time. These he called ethnic ideas.[11]

Bastian's finding corresponds to Jung's that archetypes constitute the basic themes on which different people and different cultures work out their own individual variations. Most of the time we are blissfully unaware of the existence of these basic themes, believing that our individual expressions are entirely of our own making.

The French structural anthropologist Claude Lévi-Strauss has also devoted his life to the study of cultural universals and the unconscious processes underlying them. "If, as we believe to be the case," he wrote, "the unconscious activity of the mind consists in imposing forms upon content, and if these forms are fundamentally the same for all minds — ancient or modern, primitive or civilized," then we are able to derive a principle of interpretation that is valid for all institutions and customs. The ultimate concern of Lévi-Strauss and the school of anthropology with which he is associated is with "the unconscious nature of collective phenomena." Underlying these collective phenomena, and responsible for them, are what Lévi-Strauss calls unconscious infrastructures. These are so clearly related to Jung's archetypes as to require no further comment. Yet curiously enough, Lévi-Strauss has always affected to dismiss Jung's theories. In doing so he has completely misrepresented Jung's position, as both Eugene D'Aquili and Paul Kugler have pointed out.[12]

For example, Lévi-Strauss accuses Jung of biological naïveté in identifying the archetype with psychic contents and not with the unconscious forms underlying them. In fact, Jung's position is the exact opposite of the one Lévi-Strauss arraigns him for. As Jung was writing as early as 1935: "It is necessary to point out once more that archetypes are not determined as regards their content, but only as regards their form and then only to a very limited degree. A primordial image is determined as to its content only when it has become conscious and is therefore filled out with the material of conscious experience. . . . The archetype in itself is empty and purely formal, nothing but a *facultas praeformandi.*"[13]

As Kugler tellingly observes: "Jung's description of the formal relationships in the unconscious antedates Lévi-Strauss's *Structural Anthropology* by nearly fifteen years!" Both French structuralism and Jungian psychology maintain that "the basic function of the unconscious is to impose forms (infrastructures, symbolic functions, or archetypes) upon content, especially myths, dreams, social institutions, psychopathology, and language."[14]

Among anthropologists in America, virtually the sole champions of an evolutionary approach are Robin Fox and Lionel Tiger of Rutgers University. They are contemptuous of the cultural relativism that has obsessed anthropology for most of this century. "How can we study the variables without the constants?" Fox demands. "Don't anthropologists time after time in society after society come up against the same processes carried out under a variety of symbolic disguises?" Fox's attitude is very close to Bastian's; he argues, "Once one gets behind the surface manifestations, the uniformity of human social arrangements is remarkable." Like Jung, Fox sees the human being not as a tabula rasa, but as "a bundle of potentialities." He continues, "These potentialities or predispositions or biases are the end products of a process of natural selection peculiar to the human species." Further, "man has the kinds of cultures and societies he has because he is the kind of species he is."[15]

Fox's statements strike me as axiomatic, but they have brought him nothing but contumely from his peers. However, like Jung in his lifetime, Fox continues to swim hard against the academic tide, which makes him all the more interesting as a person and as a thinker. After all, only dead fish swim constantly *with* the tide.

When the intellectual history of the twentieth century comes to be written, I believe it will be seen that the social and behavioral sciences have sadly failed to live up to their original promise. This is almost certainly because they have striven to erect a theoretical edifice on the basis of political ideology rather than evolutionary biology. To me, it is a gratifying irony that Jungian psychology can claim a more sound scientific basis than the social science that has consistently derided it, for Jungian psychology is based on an essentially biological hypothesis: the collective unconscious. The archetypes, of which the collective unconscious is composed, are biological entities; they evolved through natural selection. This is a fact of the greatest importance, for in the archetype we possess a theoretical orientation that is capable of revolutionizing not only psychology but psychiatry and anthropology as well.

What we have to do, it seems to me, is to extend Jung's work to the point where we can say with some certainty what the fundamental parameters of our archetypal potential may be and what kinds of environmental and social circumstances that potential requires if optimal personal development is to occur (or, as Jung would have put it, for individuation to proceed). Collating evidence from other disciplines is an indispensable means to furthering this objective. It is another intriguing irony that the strongest scientific support of Jung's archetypal hypothesis has come from a most surprising quarter: behavioral biology—or ethology, as it has come to be known. We must now turn to this evidence.

BEHAVIORAL BIOLOGY

In 1951, the ethologist Niko Tinbergen published a book which I have no hesitation in describing as one of the most important books of the century. It was called *The Study of Instinct*. In it he proposed that every animal species possesses a repertoire of behaviors. This behavioral repertoire is dependent upon structures evolution has built into the central nervous system of the species. Tinbergen called these structures innate releasing mechanisms, or IRMs. Each IRM is primed to become active when an appropriate stimulus — called a sign stimulus — is encountered in the environment. When such a stimulus appears, the innate mechanism is released, and the animal responds with a characteristic pattern of behavior which is adapted through evolution to the situation.[16]

When I was working on my doctoral thesis back in the 1960s, it suddenly struck me one evening that, when due allowance is made for the greater adaptive flexibility of our species, Tinbergen's position was very close to Jung's view of the nature of archetypes and their mode of activation. A mallard duck becomes amorous at the sight of a mallard drake (the green head being the sign stimulus that releases in her central nervous system the innate mechanism responsible for the characteristic patterns of behavior associated with courtship in the duck), and a ewe becomes attached to her lamb as she licks the birth membranes free of its snout. In the same way, a human mother presented with her newborn infant perceives its helplessness and its need for nurturance, and during the hours and days that follow she is overwhelmed by feelings of love, attachment, and responsibility. All such patterns of response have been prepared for by nature. As Jung himself insisted, the archetype "is not meant to denote an inherited idea, but rather an inherited mode of functioning, corresponding to the inborn way in which the chick emerges from the egg, the bird builds its nest, a certain kind of wasp stings the motor ganglion of the caterpillar, and eels find their way to the Bermudas. In other words, it is a 'pattern of behavior'. This aspect of the archetype, the purely biological one, is the proper concern of scientific psychology."[17]

Tinbergen's original ideas have been greatly extended by sociobiologists Charles Lumsden and Edward Wilson, who argue that all behavior, both human and nonhuman, depends on what they call epigenetic rules that control the psychosocial development of the individual. This idea is itself an extension of an earlier proposal by biologist C. H. Waddington that the development of all living organisms is determined by epigenetic pathways. Waddington even directly affirmed the relevance to biology of "the notion of archetypes . . . the idea, that is, that there are only a certain number of basic patterns which organic forms can assume."[18]

All these concepts—innate releasing mechanisms, patterns of behavior, epigenetic rules, and epigenetic pathways—are clearly compatible with the archetypal hypothesis Jung had proposed decades earlier to virtually universal derision. The vast wealth of the observations collected by the ethologists and the sociobiologists thus provides us with an invaluable resource with which to amplify the archetypal hypothesis and to push back the limits of our ignorance. By combing through all this material we can extract evidence that indicates how the archetypes, responsible for the crucial patterns of behavior universally present in their various forms in all mammalian and primate species, actually evolved. For in the course of human evolution, at no time have we ceased to be mammals or primates. Indeed, as neuroscientist Paul MacLean has demonstrated, the human brain incorporates still-functioning and much earlier mammalian and even reptilian brains (see Figure 1).[19] It is said, very truly, that a patient entering the consulting room brings a crowd of people along. What MacLean has shown is that the patient also brings in a horse and a crocodile!

Ethology, therefore, enables us to claim our ancient heritage not only from our hominid but from our much older ver-

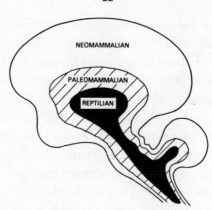

Figure 1. The Triune Brain, courtesy Paul MacLean

tebrate past. To establish for the archetype such a hallowed lineage is to put it on an unassailable scientific footing.

I should like now to look at another source of insight into archetypal functioning, namely, the study of dreams.

Dream Psychology

Freud believed that dreams weave themselves out of memory residues from two sources: from events of the previous day and from childhood. Jung accepted this, but went much further, maintaining that dreams draw on a third, much deeper source belonging to the evolutionary history of our species. It was Jung's startling and original discovery that our dreams actually grant us access to this ancient substratum of experience—that in our dreams we participate in our phylogeny. Or, to put it another way, in our dreams we speak to the species, and the species answers back.

This idea was considered fantastic when Jung proposed it, but now it is proving more acceptable. The discoveries that all mammalian species dream and that all human fetuses spend much of their time dreaming have inevitably given rise to speculation as to what on earth they can be dreaming about. Important clues have been found in sleep laboratories since Eugene Aserinsky and Nathaniel Kleitman published their revolutionary finding that dreaming is reliably correlated with REM (Rapid Eye Movement) sleep. In particular, one researcher, a Frenchman named Michel Jouvet, has made two outstanding contributions: (1) that dreams arise from bursts of activity in biologically ancient parts of the brain, and (2) that both animals and humans get up and act out their dreams when the brain centers responsible for inhibiting movements (these centers are normally active during sleep and keep us virtually paralyzed) are damaged or incapacitated. For example, dreaming cats that have had these centers removed surgically will, in their sleep, "stalk" hallucinated prey, "pounce" upon it, "kill" it, and start to "eat" it.[20]

Already, before Jouvet published his findings in the 1970s, biologists were in agreement that dreams are an essential part of our biological heritage. They declared dreams to be ancient means of adaptation, which evolved 140 million years ago. The presence of REM sleep in so many species and over so many millions of years establishes by all evolutionary criteria that dreams perform a survival function in all mammals. To account for this, it was suggested that dreams are the means by which animals update their strategies for survival by reevaluating current experience in the light of strategies formed and tested in the past. This vital work is done when the animal is asleep because it is only then that the brain is free of its outer preoccupations—rather like bank clerks doing their sums after the public is locked out and the blinds drawn down.

Jouvet carried this idea a step further. He advanced the hypothesis that in dreaming sleep an animal is updating its strategy for survival not only in the light of its own previous experience but in the light of the experience of its species. In other words, dreaming is the means by which the entire behavioral repertoire of the species is integrated with the recent experience of the individual, thus promoting its capacity to survive the demands and exigencies of the following day. What is so fascinating about Jouvet's hypothesis is that it is Jungian theory in biological dress. It exactly parallels Jung's idea that dreams compensate for one-sided attitudes of the conscious ego by mobilizing archetypal components from the collective unconscious.

There are thus good scientific reasons for supposing that dreams are, in a sense, living fossils in which we trace the primordial preoccupations of our kind. They relate the paleolithic to the present. They are biohistory incarnate, re-evoking the timeless reality implicit in the phenomenological world as we perceive it.

On the whole, it is true to say that Jung's theories have stood the test of time far better than Freud's. Thus, it is now fair to conclude that dreams are not, as Freud maintained, guardians of sleep; they are not predominantly the disguised manifestations of repressed sexual wishes; and they are not primarily responses to outer stimuli. On the contrary, they are, as Jung and Jouvet independently proposed, the result of spontaneous activity in the central nervous system and are transpersonal expressions of patterns involved with crucial life events—that is to say that they are archetypal expressions.

That these archetypal expressions should give rise to universal symbols should not, therefore, be a source of surprise. Not that Freud denied that universal symbols occur. He recognized the ubiquitousness of certain symbols not only in different fields of thought but among different civilizations and through different times.

So when Freud and Jung quarreled, the difference between them was not as to whether universal symbols occurred in dreams but as to what these universal symbols signified. Freud's reduction of them to basic sexual forms struck Jung as artificial and altogether too dogmatic. At the time, Jung had difficulty in proving his point. There were insufficient data for him to draw on to make out a convincing case for his archetypal hypothesis. Since then, innumerable dreams have been collected from members of different cultures in most regions of the world. This vast collection of material points to the truth of Jung's assertion that dream symbols are linked to all the fundamental patterns of human existence and that they reach much further in their implications than a concern with mere sexuality. Before examining some of this evidence, I should like to consider the implications of archetypal theory for contemporary psychiatry.

ARCHETYPAL PSYCHIATRY

In Book I of his celebrated *Ethics,* Aristotle postulated three levels of life: (1) the hedonic life, governed by pleasure; (2) the political life, devoted to honor and the exercise of power; and (3) the contemplative life, devoted to wisdom and truth. The first two of these are extroverted and approximate to the governing preoccupations of Freudian and Adlerian psychology, while the third is introverted and in accord with the Jungian orientation. There seems to be something of fundamental importance about these three areas of human activity, and Aristotle was not the only thinker to anticipate the great triumvirate of twentieth-century analysts. For instance, Samuel Butler observed, well over a hundred years ago, that a man's most important possessions are his religion, his money, and his private parts—again pre-empting Jung, Adler, and Freud!

As he framed it, Jung's archetypal hypothesis emerged as a fundamentally introverted concept: its extroverted implications have been explored, as we have already noted, by the anthropologists and behavioral biologists (the ethologists). In addition, some vitally important work has been carried on in this direction by a small number of ethologically oriented psychiatrists—whom I shall refer to as ethopsychiatrists, for short. The most gifted members of this select group include Brant Wenegrat and Russell Gardner in the United States and Paul Gilbert and John Price in Great Britain. Each of them has discovered and announced the existence of neuropsychic structures indistinguishable from Jungian archetypes, labeling them with their own jargon in such a way as to make them sound more scientific and more up-to-date. Wenegrat, for example, borrows the sociobiological term "genetically transmitted response strategies." These strategies are held responsible for crucial, species-specific patterns of behavior that developed in order to maximize the fitness of the organism to survive in the environment in which it evolved—what biologists call the environment of evolutionary adaptedness. These strategies are inherently shared by all members of the species, whether they be healthy or ill. Psychopathology intervenes when these strategies malfunction as a result of environmental insults or deficiencies at critical stages of development—the process I have termed "the frustration of archetypal intent."[21]

Similarly, Paul Gilbert in England dubs archetypes "psychobiological response patterns," and Russell Gardner in the United States calls them "deeply homologous neural structures." All conceive these archetypal components as dependent on genes acting as conveyors of human potential, providing individuals with the primary motives and goals typical of human beings. These genetic factors achieve healthy or unhealthy expression in response to variations in the social or physical environment, facilitating or pathogenic as the case may be.

The importance of this work is not only its extension of archetypal theory to psychiatric etiology but the historic fact that it represents the first systematic attempt to acknowledge the phylogenetic element in psychiatry and to put psychopathology on a sound evolutionary basis.

Though some ethopsychiatrists recognize their connection with Jung, most nevertheless stress their extroverted biosocial orientation, insisting that social goals are the crucial ones for psychopathology. Nearly all mental distress, in their view, is caused by difficulties experienced by the self in relation to others. We shall return to consider this work further, but at this point I should like to consider the implications of the archetypal hypothesis for the study of language and speech.

ARCHETYPAL LINGUISTICS

Have your ever stopped to consider the miraculous ease with which all children everywhere begin to speak—at an extraordinarily early age—the language, dialect, or patois spoken by the people around them in their environment? The behaviorists put this down to learning, reinforced by the reward of being understood and the punishment of not being able to ask for what you want. But you do not have to give much thought to the matter to realize that there is much more to it than mere learning. How is one to explain, for example, the amazing spurt in linguistic progress that occurs in children everywhere between eighteen and twenty-eight months of age? Why is the sequence through which linguistic functions develop similar in all children in all cultures? Why is it that toddlers playing round your seat in the Tuilleries Gardens in Paris have a virtuoso command of French vocabulary, idiom, and inflection while you, after years of study in classes and language laboratories, have difficulty in asking for a stamp?

The answer proposed by specialists in linguistics is that children are born with a brain fully equipped with the capacity for speech—with what Noam Chomsky calls a language acquisition device, which primes them to develop the knack of using words and building sentences. In other words, the acquisition of speech is archetypally determined as part of the blueprint for development that is genetically encoded in the collective unconscious of the child. Though grammars differ, their basic forms—which Chomsky calls their deep structures (yet another name for archetypes)—are universal. That is to say, at the deepest neuropsychic level, there exists a universal grammar on which all individual grammars are based.[22]

This brings us to the paradox inherent in archetypal theory: it combines the universal with the particular. In this respect, archetypes resemble Plato's ideas. For Plato, ideas were mental forms which existed above and beyond the objective world of phenomena. They were collective in the sense that they embodied the general characteristics of groups of individuals rather than the specific peculiarities of one. For example, your dog has qualities it shares in common with all dogs, which enable us to classify it as a dog. But in addition it has peculiarities of its own which enable you to pick yours out from dozens of other quadrupeds at a dog show. So it is with archetypes: they are common to all humanity, yet we all experience them in our own particular way.

It is reasonable, therefore, that a distinction should be made, as is made in French linguistics, between *langue* (language) and *parole* (speech). The point is that language is like the proverbial river: we may come and we may go, but it goes on forever. Language is a stable, collective, social institution; but each speaker of a language brings to it personal idiosyncrasies of speech; and each writer uses the language with a personal style. That is what style means.

The acquisition of language, therefore, is dependent upon the archetypal predisposition to acquire it and the existence, in the environment, of a language to acquire. To put it in the jargon of the present, if the language acquisition device is a computer, then culture provides the linguistic data the computer is programmed to process.

The purpose of this excursion into linguistics is to throw light on what occurs in dreams, for dreams have a language of their own, which enables us to speak to the species and the species to speak back to us. Like verbal language, the symbols of dream language are the products of the archetypal assimilation of experience. We can represent this thus:

Archetype + experience → symbol.

It follows that every symbol is a condensation (to use Freud's term) of the personal and the collective, the individual and the universal. The relative contribution of each differs from symbol to symbol: some symbols are so ego-referential that it is hard to recognize any archetypal contribution; others are so archetypal that one is unable to elicit any "free" associations to them.

Nancy Burson's picture entitled "Androgyne," a composite of twelve photographs, six men and six women, illustrates the point I am trying to make. There is something hauntingly familiar about it, as if it could be somebody we have known but can't quite place. It is a set of twelve variations on the archetypal theme of the human face all condensed to one image. It is this kind of condensation between the archetype and its many possible evocations which goes on every night in our dreams.[23]

Dreams are extraordinarily rich communications: they deal in feelings, intuitions, and sensations as well as thoughts. And dreams show that complex modes of apperception can be communicated just as well in images as they can in words. Indeed, images must carry precedence over words, for as any analytic session demonstrates, dream images invariably reflect more than the dreamer has previously understood or has ever attempted to express verbally. This is why dream analysis holds the central position that it does in classical Jungian therapy.

Thus, analytic practice calls into question the statements of laboratory dream researchers who insist that we can image only what we already know. There are numerous instances of scientific discovery and literary creation originating in the visual imagery of dreams: Kekulé's discovery of the benzene ring, Howe's invention of the sewing machine, and Robert Louis Stevenson's composition of *The Strange Case of Dr. Jekyll and Mr. Hyde* are probably the best-known examples. The transformative power of dreams is the work of that inner magician, the imagination. Our inventiveness is never more acute than in the creation of images. Images are the imagination at play, and it plays with the delight and ingenuity of a boisterous child. Images can suggest things that the ego would never think of. Hence Kekulé's advice: "Learn to dream."

We can see now how inadequate was Freud's understanding of the language of the unconscious as essentially primitive and infantile. To Jung, on the other hand, it was the language of Nature herself. In tune with Jung's insight, Paul Kugler in his dazzling book *The Alchemy of Discourse* seeks to establish a new discipline of archetypal linguistics—which he defines as "a linguistics of the poetic imagination." Stating his manifesto, he declares, "Archetypal linguistics is the speech of the soul."[24]

The language of dreams is, as George Orwell might have put it, nature-speak, for nature speaks to us directly in dreams and myths. In our dreams we enter the natural world of our kind: it is the archetypal world, and the archetypal world is the natural world of the dreamer. In dreams we enter the paleolithic caves of our ancestors, and, God help them, bring them up-to-date.

What do our ancestors make of the contemporary world? Much of it, I suspect, they rather like—the ready availability of food, drink, comfort, entertainment, and sexual gratification. But they miss the close ties of kinship, the intimacy of small-community life, the shared responsibilities of hunting, gathering, and defense, the working interaction with nature, the rites and rituals, the myths and legends of heroes, gods, and goddesses, and the magical sense of living in an animated world. Sometimes the disparity between their world and ours is more than they can bear, and they break down and become ill. We shall return to this theme.

ENTERING PREHISTORY

Jung's own anthropological researches in the 1920s, his visits to Algeria and Tunisia, Kenya and Uganda and to the Pueblo Indians of New Mexico, were much more than intellectual tourism. They were part of his need to achieve the self-realization of the unconscious, and they brought him into contact with what he called the two million-year-old within. Of his visit to North Africa he wrote: "Just as a childhood memory can suddenly take possession of consciousness with so lively an emotion that we feel wholly transported back to the original situation, so the seemingly alien and wholly different Arab surroundings awaken an archetypal memory of an only too well known pre-historic past which apparently we have entirely forgotten. We are remembering a potentiality of life which has been overgrown by civilization, but which in certain places is still existent."[25] Unfortunately, the number of places in which it is still existent have dwindled to such a drastic extent since Jung visited them that there are precious few of them left.

Having entered the archetypal realm during his confrontation with the unconscious between 1914 and 1918, he sought during the 1920s to corroborate his introverted researches from the outside, throwing objective light on the prehistoric layers of collective experience and potential: "I unconsciously wanted to find that part of my personality which had become invisible under the influence and the pressure of being European."[26]

Apart from providing valuable insights into the age-old patterns of human life, these journeys provided him with a standpoint from which he could take a more objective view of Western civilization. It confirmed his impression that Europeans had become alienated from their own humanity. Because their rationalism had been won at the expense of their vitality, the more primitive nature of Europeans had been "condemned to a more or less underground existence." His travels made Jung deeply aware of his consanguinity with the people he encountered, and he came to believe that Europeans despised primitive peoples in order to defend themselves against the recognition of how spiritually impoverished, how lacking in animal vitality they were by comparison. "Knowledge does not enrich us," he wrote; "it removes us more and more from the mythic world in which we were once at home by right of birth."[27]

In particular, he was overcome by a powerful sense of déjà vu on his arrival in Kenya, when he was traveling from Mombassa to Nairobi and saw a tribesman standing on a rocky promontory in the early morning sun.

When the first ray of sunlight announced the onset of day, I awoke. The train, swathed in a red cloud of dust, was just making a turn around a steep red cliff. On a jagged rock above us a slim, brownish-black figure stood motionless, leaning on a long spear, looking down at the train. Beside him towered a gigantic candelabrum cactus.

I was enchanted by this sight—it was a picture of something utterly alien and outside my experience, but on the other hand a most intense *sentiment du déjà vu*. I had the feeling that I had already experienced this moment and had al-

ways known this world which was separated from me only
by distance in time. It was as if I were this moment returning to the land of my youth, and as if I knew that dark-
skinned man who had been waiting for me for five thousand
years.

The feeling-tone of this curious experience accompanied
me throughout my whole journey through savage Africa.

Jung concluded: "I could not guess what string within myself
was plucked at the sight of that solitary dark hunter. I knew
only that his world had been mine for countless millennia."[28]

He traveled to the north of Nairobi to the slopes of Mount
Elgon to stay among the Elgonyi. There he experienced complete happiness. "Our camp life proved to be one of the loveliest
interludes of my life. I enjoyed the 'divine peace' of a still primeval country. . . . My liberated psychic forces poured blissfully
back to the primeval expanses."[29]

He had come home. This was his world. When the time
for departure came, he could barely tear himself away and swore
that he would come back at the first opportunity. When he
did eventually return, ten years later, it was to find that this
previously pristine Eden had been transformed into a gold mine.
The timeless world of beauty, passion, and spirit was no longer
accessible.[30] Such are the crippling and disfiguring wounds our
century has everywhere inflicted.

Jung never forgot a conversation that he had with an Elgonyi medicine man, who told him that the Elgonyi had always
paid great attention to their dreams, which guided them in all
the important decisions of their lives. But now, the old man
added sadly, his people no longer needed their dreams because
the English, who ruled the earth (this was the 1920s, remember), knew everything, and dreams were therefore no longer
necessary.

Jung saw parallels in the cultural patterns of peoples wherever he traveled. In America, for example, he was fascinated by the way in which the initiation ceremonies of American college fraternities directly resembled those of American Indian tribes; that the deadly seriousness with which modern Americans played their sports embodied the heroic ideal of the Native American; and that the rituals of secret societies such as the Ku Klux Klan and the Knights of Columbus resembled the practices of American Indian mystery religions. Jung believed that immigrant Americans had been influenced by the traditions of the indigenous population to a much more profound degree than they realized. Not only did Christian Science echo American Indian shamanism in its beliefs and modes of healing, but the skylines of Chicago and New York, the "houses piling up in towers towards the centre," were just like those of the Indian pueblos of the Southwest. "Without conscious imitation," commented Jung, the American unconsciously fills out the spectral outline of the Red Man's mind and temperament."[31]

Jung's expeditions were symbolic journeys as well as field trips. They were yet another descent into the underworld in search of the treasure hard to attain. For Jung, as all his writings make abundantly clear, the unconscious was no mere concept to be studied in academic seclusion: it was a demon possessing immense authority and overwhelming energy of its own. It was something to be confronted, grappled with, and contained. Hence his designation of the individuation process as the *opus contra naturam*. The unconscious is nature, but we have to confront its contents if we are to become conscious of them.

His own confrontation with the unconscious brought him face to face with two archetypal figures: the anima (Salome) and the wise old man (Philemon). While he was to spend much time later in researching both these figures in the literature of myth, religion, and alchemy, it is typical of him that his primary knowledge of them was derived from direct personal experience: gnosis. The rest was mere circumambulation. To Jung, true knowledge was, and had to be, revelatory.

So, as Jung knew, we may increase our intellectual understanding of the archetype by studying all the different sources of knowledge about it, but if we wish to *experience* its vitalizing energy, then we have to risk making ourselves vulnerable to the influence of the primordial survivor in our own lives.

2.

Dreaming Myths

Not for a moment dare we succumb to the illusion that an archetype can be finally explained and disposed of. . . . The most we can do is to dream the myth onwards *and give it a modern dress.*
— C. G. Jung, *Collected Works*, vol. 9, part 1

A myth is a public dream, a dream is a private myth.
— Joseph Campbell

There are certain areas of agreement between Jungian psychology and behavioral biology, with particular reference to the role of the collective unconscious and the function of dreams. The ethological view that dreaming sleep is necessary for an animal to update its strategies for survival by integrating the ethogram (the total behavioral repertoire of the species encoded in the brain) with the recent experience of the individual is in close accord with the Jungian view, proposed forty years earlier, that our dreams nightly put us in touch with the wisdom of the two million-year-old human being who exists as living potential within the collective unconscious of us all.

In strictly biological terms, dreams are genetically determined behavioral rehearsals which, like play, prepare the organism for the eventualities of daily life. Thus, we can translate Alfred Adler's insight that "dreams are dress rehearsals for life" into the terminology of contemporary ethology—namely, that dreams play an indispensable role in organizing the ethogram (in our terms, the archetypal program for life) into the complicated behavioral and psychic sequences involved in the crucial life performances of all mammals, such as courtship, mating, hunting, dominance striving, and territorial acquisition and defense.

That phylogenetically ancient structures play an important part in the dreams of human beings can be deduced from statistical studies that focus on the content of dreams. In one study of the common dreams of college students, for example, the following themes were reported, in descending order of frequency: falling, being pursued or attacked, repeated attempts at performing a task, experiences connected with academic work, and sex.[1] All these types of dreams, with the exception of those concerned with academic work, have fairly evident phylogenetic links. It is not surprising, for example, that a creature which in earlier stages of its evolution spent much of its life in trees should experience anxiety dreams of falling. Similarly, nightmares of being pursued or attacked are to be expected in a species whose primordial conflicts have involved hunting, fighting, and striving for dominance. Furthermore, the vital need to master changes in the environment, to acquire physical skills, perform religious and social rituals, and so on require repeated attempts to learn and perform such tasks. Finally, the contribution of sexual behavior to the survival of the species requires no comment.

Calvin S. Hall and Vernon J. Nordby, those intrepid collectors of dreams in the 1950s and 1960s, also concluded, on the basis of their examination of more than fifty thousand dreams, that a number of typical themes are repeated over and over again. By a theme they meant the same basic plot or event. "This is true for individual dream series as well as for sets of dreams obtained from groups of people," they wrote. "These *typical dreams,* as we shall call them, are experienced by virtually every dreamer, although there are differences in the frequency with which these dreams occur among individual dreamers and among groups of dreamers."[2]

The typical dreams reported by Hall and Nordby involved aggression, predatory animals, flying, falling, being pursued by hostile strangers, landscapes, dreams of misfortune, sex, getting married and having children, taking examinations or undergoing some similar ordeal, traveling (whether on foot, horseback, car, airplane, or ship), swimming or being in the water, watching fires, and being confined in an underground place. "All people living in Western civilization will have these dreams at some time in their lives," they wrote, "and many of them will be repeated again and again." Though Freudian by orientation, Hall and Nordby concluded: "These typical dreams express the shared concerns, preoccupations, and interests of all dreamers. They may be said to constitute the universal constants of the human psyche."[3] Dreams thus provide us with copious evidence in support of Jung's hypothesis of the collective unconscious.

One of Hall and Nordby's more interesting findings is that "many more bad things than good things happen to the dreamer in his dreams. . . . We infer from it that people conceive of the world as a predominantly threatening, unfriendly, hostile place."[4] This conflicts sharply with the Freudian view that dreams are disguised wish fulfillments. And although they don't make this interpretation, their finding is susceptible to the biological explanation that one function of dreams is to alert and prepare the dreamer to encounter the kind of threats that were usual in the environment of evolutionary adaptedness (that is to say, the environment in which our species evolved and in which we have lived for 99 percent of our existence).

Although Hall and Nordby insist that their research is uninfluenced by Freudian assumptions, these assumptions are never-theless apparent. For example, they interpret dreams in which predatory animals with big teeth pursue the dreamer as castra-tion dreams. They do not for one moment consider the possi-bility that such dreams could be phylogenetically determined. One dream that they cite as a castration dream in fact expresses the archetypes of landscape, predation, and escape. A young man reported the following: I dreamed that I was in a large open space and huge animals of all sorts with wide open mouths and big gnashing teeth were chasing me. I ran from side to side trying to escape. The huge animal monsters finally hemmed me in. They were going to claw and eat me. I awoke."[5]

From the point of view of Jungian psychology, the finding of most interest is that certain symbols occur again and again in dreams of people from differing cultural and linguistic back-grounds. At about the time that Hall and Nordby were con-ducting their research, a fascinating study by Dr. Richard Griffith in the United States in association with Drs. O. Miyagi and A. Tago in Japan compared the dreams of 250 college students in Kentucky and 223 in Tokyo. More than seven thousand dreams were collected, and when they were examined to discover how often certain themes recurred, it was found that remarkable simi-larity existed between the two groups. Moreover, the recurrent themes detected are very similar to those described by Hall and Nordby.[6]

It seems that dreams return repeatedly to those themes— we would call them archetypal themes—which have typically concerned human beings always and everywhere. Again Jung's axiom is confirmed: "Ultimately, every individual life is at the same the eternal life of the species."[7]

What is crucial to the survival of every mammalian species is that basic reflex processes (what ethologists call fixed action patterns) become efficiently organized into appropriate behavior in the course of ontological development. The basic four F's of fixed action are feeding, fighting, fleeing, and fornication. If Michel Jouvet is right and REM sleep is indeed a "genetically determined behaviour rehearsal," then the vital significance of dreams is that they enable the animal to respond appropriately to food, threat, attack, and sexual encounters even before the gustatory, threatening, or erotic stimuli are encountered. As J. Allan Hobson puts it in his indispensable book *The Dreaming Brain,* the neural program for behavioral acts must be put in place before certain behavior is demanded.[8]

Hobson reports an incident from his own experience which convinced him that this must be so, and that we are indeed prepared by our dreams and by our heredity to defend ourselves and to fight even if we have never been trained to do so. "Three men once cornered me in the parking lot where I had parked my car," he writes.

> It was early one spring morning, and I was going to the lab to monitor a sleep-lab experiment. All of my wit and wile were unsuccessful in protecting me from assault. Only after I had been knocked to the ground unconscious, and was being kicked and pummelled, did some primordial urge rise up within me. I remember feeling what seemed at the time to be inhuman strength, probably surges of adrenal hormone. I threw the three men off and, with two of them chasing me, ran with Olympic speed up an alley. I recall that, at the peak of my aggressive strength, I thought, "these men want to kill me."
>
> Where did this primordial surge of aggressive energy and strength come from? This particular set of behaviors had never before emerged, yet I was somehow capable of it. I certainly did not have time to learn it on the spot! I would not deny the value of childhood and adolescent play and the ritualized aggressive games of boyhood; but to look back even further,

my guess is that the brain basis of many of these acts had been put in place and maintained over time for just such an occasion. It did not save my nose (which was broken into smithereens), but it did save my life.[9]

Hobson comments that, as with aggression, the sexual act is dependent upon fixed-action patterns that have a life of their own, and are, apparently, in constant readiness so that, even after long fallow periods, an erotic encounter can result in instant performance. This fact could have reassured Oscar Hammerstein II, who married early. His future father-in-law demanded to know if he was a virgin, and Hammerstein readily asserted that he was. "You mean you're going to practice on my daughter?" retorted the irate parent. His anxiety was probably unnecessary. REM sleep erections and wet dreams, particularly in puberty or adolescence, are outward signs of the role played by dreaming in the activation and maintenance of the psycho-physical infrastructures responsible for sexual experience and behavior. As we know, it was this aspect of dreaming that was of primary interest to Freud, who overemphasized its significance and attempted to subsume all dream activity under its influence.

Hobson's suggestions, like those of Jouvet, are entirely compatible with Jungian theory. And although Paul MacLean proposed his concept of the triune brain several years after Jung's death, Jung had already anticipated it, maintaining that dreams about mammals or reptiles related to phylogenetically ancient mammalian and reptilian structures in the brain and were expressions of the deeper intentions of nature itself. "The evolutionary stratification of the psyche," wrote Jung, "is more clearly discernible in the dream than in the conscious mind. In the dream, the psyche speaks in images, and gives expression to instincts, which derive from the most primitive levels of nature. Therefore, through the assimilation of unconscious contents, the momentary life of consciousness can once more be brought into harmony with the law of nature from which it all too easily departs, and the patient can be led back to the natural law of his own being."[10]

Our difficulties, neurotic, psychotic, psychopathic, or otherwise, Jung argued, "come from losing contact with our instincts, with the age-old unforgotten wisdom stored up in us. And where do we make contact with this old man in us? In our dreams."[11] Dreams, therefore, are the language used in the lifelong dialogue proceeding nightly between the ego and the unconscious: they are the means by which the individual becomes psychically related to the life cycle of the species.

The truth of this statement becomes clear when we examine a long series of dreams from the same dreamer. Each individual dream is an act of compensation, "a momentary adjustment of one-sidedness or an equalization of disturbed balance. But with deeper insight and experience," wrote Jung, "these apparently separate acts of compensation arrange themselves into a kind of plan. They seem to hang together and in the deepest sense to be subordinated to a common goal, so that a long dream-series no longer appears as a senseless string of incoherent and isolated happenings, but resembles the successive steps in a planned and orderly process of development. I have called this unconscious process spontaneously expressing itself in the symbolism of a long dream-series the individuation process."[12]

A Dream Interpreted

Let us now look at a dream and interpret it in the light of what I have been saying. Gary, a farmer in his early thirties, had this dream:

"It was a golden evening of late summer. A feeling of great

ripeness was in the air. The landscape glimmered in the sharp evening light with an intensity that struck me as supernatural. I stood in the yard behind our farmhouse waiting for someone to return from the fields after a day's harvesting.

"Suddenly, I hear the sound of a tractor coming down the lane. An elderly man—I think my father—is at the wheel. As he approaches the big seventeenth-century gate piers marking the entrance to the farm, I notice my Uncle John lurking in the shadows of a nearby chestnut tree. In his hand he holds the broadsword, dating from the [English] Civil War, which normally hangs in the hall of the farm. To my horror, I realize he means to attack my father. I try to cry out and run towards him, but some force paralyzes me and I can't shout and I can't move. Feeling totally helpless and impotent, I watch in anguish as my uncle leaps onto the tractor and drags the elderly figure (who is now clearly my father) from the driving seat, throwing him to the ground. Then with sickening brutality, Uncle begins to hack at him with the sword. 'Stop!' I scream, but the word gets no further than a gurgle in my throat. A dreadful sadness takes hold of me as I realize that my father can never survive this terrible assault.

"Then I am with a woman in a woodland nearby. It's nearly dark. Somehow she knows what has happened and tries to console me. She is like my fiancée, but darker and taller and older, a bit like my mother in fact. She tells me I must never forget what I have seen and must spend my life putting it right.

"I wake feeling drained, full of disturbed emotions. My heart thuds loudly and I fear I'm having a heart attack. This passes but the dream disturbs me for the rest of the day."

In working together on this dream, Gary and I approached it in the classic Jungian manner. That is to say, I asked him to do some active imagination—to dream the dream onwards, so to speak—and also to provide his personal associations to the events and personalities in the dream. We then examined the cultural and archetypal backgrounds to the dream and shared, as fully as possible, the insights and feelings that emerged. Let us take each of these stages in turn.

Active imagination: The first thought that struck Gary was that his uncle was a survivor; he could always justify and get away with anything he did, however shady, so there is no question of his owning up to the crime or facing up to the consequences of his terrible action. Since John had no idea that his attack had been observed, his first concern was burial of his brother's remains in a place where they would not be discovered. Gary said, "I can hear his voice saying, 'A murderer's first concern is to get rid of the body.'"

Personal associations: Gary's father, Andrew, was the oldest of his siblings, and being the eldest, inherited the family farm when Gary's grandfather was killed in a tractor accident at the age of sixty-three. Andrew's brother John (the dreamer's uncle) was only a year younger than Andrew, and an intense rivalry had always existed between them. Although John's senior, Andrew was more sensitive, slighter of build, and less aggressive. As a boy, John had quickly learned to use his size and greater physical strength to intimidate Andrew and made little secret of the fact that he despised his elder brother. Moreover, John had always been their father's favorite, and when the older man was killed, John bitterly resented the fact that it was Andrew who inherited the farm and not he. To add insult to injury, he considered Andrew to be totally unworthy of his position. For unlike John, Andrew was very "green": he hated to use chemicals on the land and would have nothing to do with mechanized farming of animals. John, on the other hand, advocated the use of all the very latest scientific discoveries to maximize profits and productivity, as his father had left him an interest in the farm.

So what did this family conflict mean to the dreamer? Gary loved his father and rather feared his uncle, but he had to admit that there were times when his father seemed misguided and it was true that the farm was going downhill financially. Gary had often been present when rows flared up between his father and uncle, and latterly he had come to feel that his uncle was getting the better of the argument. However, his father stubbornly refused to be moved from his principled position. In the past, Gary had kept quiet during these rows, but increasingly he felt he should intervene and support some of the proposals advanced by his Uncle John. Gary worried about the effect this intervention would have on his father and was in considerable conflict about this at the time of his dream.

The dream clearly represents this conflict in the dreamer. It is as if he realizes that by siding with his uncle he would in fact be killing his father. That the sword dates from the Civil War reflects the nature of the war taking place within the family and within the dreamer's psyche. That the ego is paralyzed and unable to intervene may be due to the actual paralysis experienced by everyone in REM sleep, but it could also symbolize the emotional paralysis experienced by Gary in waking reality when he confronts the conflict between his two seniors.

The dream is telling him that if he resolves the conflict by adopting the attitude of his uncle, he must be prepared to kill both his actual father and his inner father (i.e., that part of himself that is identified with his father's attitude and personality).

The female figure, in part his fiancée, in part his mother, is *au fond* his anima. She understands the profound significance of this masculine conflict and tells him that he will have to spend his life resolving it. This is true enough, since Gary will himself run and later inherit the farm as his father passes on into old age and death. There is also a death wish implicit in the dream: his father is on a tractor, and it was on a tractor that his father's father died.

Now all this seems clear and straightforward enough, and I imagine that most schools and analysis would go along with what I have said about the dream so far, though they would probably stress some details more than others. For example, Freudians would doubtless call attention to the sword as a phallic symbol, pointing out that through his closer relationship and identity with his father, Uncle John possessed greater phallic power than father Andrew and consequently symbolized this power in the psyche of the dreamer. Also the uncle's murderous action represents the parricide in Gary—his desire to slay the father and inherit the kingdom (i.e., the tractor association). Freudians would doubtless interpret this Oedipally, especially in view of the resemblance between Gary's anima and his mother. What would a Jungian add to this? Inevitably, the cultural and the archetypal dimensions.

Cultural associations: The seventeenth-century farmhouse, the gate piers, and the broadsword are all contemporaneous with the English Civil War (1642–46). Like all civil wars it was about power: who rules? The King or Parliament? Oliver Cromwell cuts off King Charles's head and usurps his power. Cromwell's government is eventually removed and the King's son restored, but he is now a constitutional monarch who rules with the consent of parliament and the people.

This history provides Gary with an allegory of what is happening in his own case: he is in the process of becoming a constitutional monarch who succeeds to the strife-torn kingdom ravaged by the struggle between his father (the King) and his uncle (Cromwell).

Archetypal associations: Are there any parallels to this drama in mythology? Indeed there are! Many of them. The myth which leaps most immediately to mind, almost in its entirety,

is that of Osiris. Osiris is far and away the most appealing of
the Egyptian gods. The peaceful bringer of civilization, he taught
people how to cultivate grain and the vine and to make bread,
beer, and wine. He built the first cities and temples and gave
all these benefits to the known world, together with the de-
lights of music and the arts. All this was achieved without violence but with goodwill and by example.

But, alas, this is an imperfect world. Osiris has a jealous
brother, Set, who wishes to seize power from Osiris and put
it to his own egocentric ends. Together with a gang of accom-
plices, Set kidnaps Osiris, nails him up in a wooden coffer, and
casts him into the Nile. The coffer is carried out to sea and
across the Byblos on the Phoenician coast, where it comes to
rest at the foot of a tamarisk tree.

Enter Osiris's wife, his sister Isis. She goes to Phoenicia and
recovers the body of Osiris. To deceive Set, she hides it in the
swamp of the Nile Delta. But there it is discovered by Set one
night when he is out hunting by moonlight. Set attacks the
body with his knife, dismembering it into fourteen pieces, which
he then scatters far and wide.

Not to be outwitted, Isis seeks out the precious fragments
and collects them together, except for one very important part:
the phallus. She reassembles the pieces and, for the first time
in history, performs the rites of embalmment, which restore
the murdered god to eternal life. The phallus is replaced by the
Djed pillar, symbol of eternal generativity.

Osiris is an example of the Great Individual, the Anthropos,
and can be understood as representing humankind and the total
archetypal endowment of the Self. He is the embodiment of
that creative genius in our species which transformed the hunter-
gatherer into the civilized agriculturalist. He also represents the
principle of death and rebirth, for he is a vegetation spirit ani-
mating the corn, the vine, and the trees.

48

Set is altogether different. If Osiris is the Self in all its life-enhancing creativity, then Set is the grasping ego, high-jacking Osiris's power for his own greedy and destructive purposes. It is significant that Set was not born naturally. He tore his way violently out of his mother's womb. Moreover, he had white skin and red hair, both of which the Egyptians disliked, especially the latter which they compared to the pelt of an ass. So Set is a kind of prefiguration of Nordic man, who does violence to nature to satisfy his own ego-needs.

The parallels between the Osiris myth and Gary's dream are so striking as to require little comment. The dream casts Gary's father in the role of Osiris, his Uncle John in the role of Set, and his mother/fiancée/anima in the role of Isis.

That the quarrel between the two brothers is over two contrary modes of farming—the organic and the technological—merely means that the myth has been brought up-to-date. In this dream Gary has produced a contemporary myth, his own myth, tailor-made for our times.

A further mythological parallel to the relationship between Gary's father and his Uncle John is that between Prometheus ("he who knows in advance") and his brother Epimetheus ("he who learns after the event"). Prometheus stole fire from the gods to compensate humanity for the prodigal stupidity of his brother, who dissipated the gifts of the gods and left humanity with few resources. For his brave act of defiance, the gods punished Prometheus by binding him to the Caucasus and sending an eagle to feed on his liver every day. They also sent Epimetheus the beautiful but treacherous Pandora, who brought death and destruction into the world.

This myth tells in different guise the story of the Fall. By defying the gods, the man becomes conscious of the laws of nature and subjugates them to his will. Emerging from the hunter-gatherer state, he seizes all the goods of the world for his own gratification. Epimetheus is an impulsive *bon viveur* who, like Set, has no concern for the morrow. His motto is Eat, drink, and be merry, for tomorrow we die.

Needless to say, Gary had never heard of Osiris, and, although he knew of Prometheus's gift of fire to humanity, he had no idea of Epimetheus's part in this sad history. When I told him of these things, he was visibly shaken and sat silent in his chair for five minutes before he could trust himself to speak.

The outcome of this dream, and our work on it, was that his entire understanding of the conflict both inside and outside himself was transformed, and he was enabled in one session to see a way forward, which transcended the polar standpoints adopted by his father and his uncle. This also had the effect of furthering his personal growth and individuation.

By relating the dream to its mythic context, Gary was suddenly able to see that his intrapsychic drama was part of the greater drama being played out on a global scale, and this thought allied him in renewed sympathy with his father's cause, giving it a metaphysical, almost religious intensity. In Western civilization, Osiris lies slumbering in the depths of the collective unconscious, a sleep so profound as to resemble coma, while in the collective conscious Set is both in command and on the rampage. Set has no time for the eternal cycles of nature or for a civilized adjustment to them: he subverts everything to his own selfish needs in the here and now, with no concern for ecology or the morrow. When the bulldozers move in to rip up the countryside, Set is at the wheel. When a thousand square miles of rain forest are to be laid waste, Set lights the fire. When a multitude of Iraqi conscripts is to be incinerated on the road from Kuwait City, Set is at the controls. For Set puts himself against the laws of nature, and like all true outlaws, rapes and pillages with no thought of the consequences. Set is an ecological psychopath, and in our world he rules. Put in psychological terms, Set is the selfish ego divorced from the selfless Self. For what we do to the environment is a direct consequence of what we do to ourselves. "There is only one thing wrong with the world," said Jung, "and that is man."[13]

Gary serves as a good example to us all because he demonstrates a means of healing the split between the ego and the Self, so that Set and Osiris may be reconciled: we should attend with great seriousness to our dreams; dreams are the pillow talk of the ego and Self. Essentially, this is an alchemical conversation because dreams are the *prima materia* of our psychic life. In the interaction of conscious with unconscious, personal with archetypal, a magical transformation occurs, and the quest for psychic wholeness is brought a stage nearer. Attention to such dialogues on a nightly basis can alter how we perceive our role in life and how we deal with the world about us.

Before we pass on to other matters, let us consider a few more parallels to Gary's dream. The drama of Set and Osiris is anticipated by the Sumerian epic of Gilgamesh and Enkidu, which dates from the dawn of history. Enkidu, is the embodiment of nature and the Self, and he grows up in the wilderness with animals for his companions. On the other hand, Gilgamesh, King of Uruk, the first great city of the world, with its ramparts and enormous wealth, is the heroic ego who casts off the ancient modesty of the hunter-gatherer living in harmonious balance with his surroundings and by a bold exertion of his will, slays the monster Humbaba and lays waste the great forest of cedar trees stretching from the Lebanon to the Euphrates. He coerces Enkidu into assisting him in this gigantic task—displaying the discipline, determination, and iron will through which the ego can so successfully annex the energies of the Self and put them to the service of its own inflated ambitions.

> For the King of Ramparted Uruk
> Has altered the unalterable way,
> Abused, changed the practices.[14]

The words speak to us of a truth even more familiar now than when they were impressed on the ancient clay tablets all those thousands of years ago. Great civilizations come and go, but the human psyche goes on grappling with the same issues, generation after generation.

The aggressive power-hunger of the hero—Gilgamesh, Heracles, Odysseus—is always balanced by figures carrying the opposite values of peace, love, and attachment to the divine, as Frank Cawson points out in an important manuscript on the hero archetype, "The Hero Must Die." Instead of a weapon, Dionysus carries a wand sprouting an ivy leaf, Orpheus strums his lute, Christ holds a shepherd's crook, while the Buddha sits in quiet meditation, his hands open and unarmed. Contrast with these Heracles, shouldering his great phallic club ("every weapon of war, from Heracles' club to the nuclear bomb and Scud missile, replicates the shape and something of the mechanism of the phallus," says Cawson)[15] and Odysseus with his enormous stake putting out the eye of Polyphemus, the Cyclops, who like all his kind lives in ignorance of civilization, incapable of agriculture and organized productivity, inhabiting a pre-Fall Eden, depending entirely on the bounty of nature. Telling us of these creatures, Homer sings:

> . . . . they neither plow
> nor sow by hand, nor till the ground, though grain—
> wild wheat and barley—grow untended, and
> wine-grapes, in clusters, ripen in heaven's rain.[16]

The symbolism of Odysseus's act in blinding Polyphemus is a violent piece of psychic repression, rendering the creature of nature unconscious.

The problem of Set, Gilgamesh, and the rest, also appears in the second part of Goethe's *Faust*. Mephistopheles is the dealer, procurer, entrepreneur, who can get you anything you want — provided you sell your soul to the devil. The theme also surfaces in art, as in Bruegel's great picture *The Fall of Icarus* in the Musée des Beaux Arts, in Brussels. And again, in the numerous representations of the warrior-hero on his horse.

The hero's association with the horse is richly symbolic of his whole attitude to natural things. A beautiful creature of elemental power, of speed and grace, the horse is something to be captured, possessed, mastered, and exploited. The hero harnesses it to his chariot, shackles its mouth, breaks it in, whips it, forces it to obey his will. Alexander the Great, riding Bucephalus, conquers the known world from Macedonia to the Hindu Kush and beyond; Genghis Khan and his marauding gang of bloodthirsty heroes gallop across the Steppes of Asia, looting, pillaging, raping, murdering, spreading terror and misery wherever it pleases them to go. Horse breaking can stand as a symbol for what the masculine ego does to nature when it goes after fame, fortune, and the other Fs in the hero's vocabulary.

As the warrior-hero treats his horses, so he treats his women (and the feminine in himself). The anima is rigorously repressed, as it is in the training of young soldiers to this day. There can be no place for gentleness or compassion when killing's to be done. "The greatest happiness for a man," declared Genghis Khan, "and the greatest joy, is to defeat and exterminate the enemy, to destroy him in his very roots, to take all he possesses, to force his wives to weep, to ride his best and beloved horses, and to have the joy of possessing his beautiful women." Women are objects to be enjoyed as much out of a sadistic desire to humiliate their menfolk as out of the urge for sexual gratification.

Yet even in the hero, the Self still works to express all its potential in life, including relationship with the feminine. Eventually, the most warlike Mars will seek his Venus, Ares his Aphrodite. Odysseus returns to Ithaca to drive out the suitors and be reunited with Penelope. Usually, the anima has to wait for the warrior to weary of his material conquests before she can contrive to conquer him.

In Gary's case, however, there was no such waiting. The anima was alive to his problem, and when he shared his dream experience with his fiancée, she understood: it confirmed many feelings she had been keeping to herself. She was able to pledge him her loyal support as his consort and future queen, and the bond was strengthened between them.

As all this amplification serves to prove, Gary's dream was a "big" dream touching on profound archetypal themes and carrying great numinous power. It was a culture pattern dream. All dreams have implicit in them some archetypal component, but some dreams are more evidently archetypal than others, in that they are different — uncanny and eerie. They stir up the dreamer's feelings because they bring up the most important issues of life and death. Such dreams are private myths.

DREAM ECOLOGY

Before we leave Gary's dream altogether, I should say something about the landscape in which the drama unfolds. It is the familiar landscape of Gary's ordinary working life, yet in the dream it is "a golden evening of late summer," and the fields and hedgerows glow with an intensity that strikes him as supernatural.

There is more than a hint of the Virgilian Golden Age in this description, the innocence of Eden before the Fall. The desire to evoke this paradise and lament its loss is the intention behind much poetry (William Wordsworth, Thomas Hardy, Gerard Manley Hopkins, A. E. Housman), music (Frederick Delius, Edward Elgar, Ralph Vaughan Williams), and art

(Claude, Poussin, Constable, the Impressionists). Many would attribute such nostalgia to a fantasied idealization of childhood; but it clearly goes deeper than this, for such intense feelings begin early in childhood itself, presumably because children live so much closer to the archetypal realm of experience and so inhabit an *animated* world. Animals, plants, trees, streams, the wind, all are alive and self-aware, relished through a *participation mystique* of projective identification. Children share that "nature mysticism" common to all primal peoples, which the Romantic poets elevated into an aesthetic device and which Jung discovered as a boy sitting on a stone in his father's garden ("Am I the one who is sitting on the stone, or am I the stone on which *he* is sitting?").[17]

One has but to make the effort of imagination to remember what it was like. As a child, I would look at a prospect of fields, woods, hills, and streams, marvel at the vivid variety of color, the dancing glints of light on leaves and water, and wonder, "Did it look like this in the eighteenth century?" A glow of delight would come with the answer, "Yes, it did." Years afterwards I wondered what that was about. I am sure that it was a glimpse of the timeless world—the world as our ancestors have always seen it. The sense that it is not "I" here perceiving this landscape as a private film show, but the primordial survivor gazing upon it through my eyes. At such moments I became vividly, transcendentally alive, inspired with a heightened awareness of unique selfhood within an eternally human context.

Landscape is numinous to us in dreams and waking reality because it is, to use Jung's phrase, born in us as a virtual image: it is an archetypal given, so to speak. In his childhood, Gary came to know and love every acre of meadow and woodland that had belonged to his family for nearly four hundred years. One reason why he sympathized so powerfully with his father

was that it caused him physical pain to think of the brutal transformations that full mechanization would bring. The sense of
continuity was precious to him, and the idea that it all could
change was intolerable.

Here, too, he shared in a collective predicament — one which
we in England have endured since the beginning of the Industrial Revolution but which people in America, with its wide-
open spaces, are only just beginning to comprehend. The nine-
teenth-century poets and painters warned us that what we were
doing to our landscape would ultimately destroy our souls. Hopkins's poem *Inversnaid* is a poignant example:

> What would the world be, once bereft
> Of wet and of wildness? Let them be left,
> O let them be left, wildness and wet:
> Long live the weeds and the wilderness yet.

In the past, places changed so slowly that we could return
to the scenes of our childhood for intimations of permanence
and eternity. This is becoming increasingly difficult. Like a
George Orwell hero searching for the magical pond where as
a boy he saw an enormous carp, we find nothing but a shopping mall, a housing development, or an industrial estate. It
seems that one of the unavoidable pains of growing older in
the contemporary world is the anguish of loss — the willfull destruction of what one knew and loved as a child. The result
is alienating, enraging, bereaving. One has lost not only a beloved corner of the earth but a precious part of one's humanity.
The primordial survivor weeps.

> Into my heart an air that kills
> From yon far country blows.
> What are those blue remembered hills
> What spires, what farms are those?

56

That is the land of lost content,
I see it shining plain,
The happy highways where I went
And cannot come again.

—A. E. Housman

Later I shall argue that the forces in the contemporary world which are hostile to nature are also hostile to our dreams, and that we will continue to maltreat our environment as long as we maltreat ourselves. As far as Nature is concerned, inner and outer, psyche and matter are all one. No Cartesian dualist, she!

3.

The Healing Wound

We, each and all of us, contain within us the entire history of the world, and just as our body records Man's genealogy as far back as the fish and then some, so our soul encompasses everything that has ever existed in human souls. All gods and devils that have ever existed are within us as possibilities, as desires, as solutions.
—HERMANN HESSE, *Reflections*

ALL MY PROFESSIONAL LIFE, I've been interested in a subject that has conspicuously failed to engage the great majority of psychologists, social scientists, and historians throughout this century—namely, the evolution of the unconscious psyche. This preoccupation reaches a peak for me, as it did for Jung, in the psychobiology of mental disorder. I shall focus now on the ways in which mental illness can afflict us when the two million-year-old human being within becomes frustrated, frightened, or discontented.

In *Memories, Dreams, Reflections,* Jung records that when he entered the psychiatric profession—to the dismay of his tutors and fellow students—it was because he realized that psychiatry was the one branch of medicine which embraced the two passionate interests of his life: nature and the life of the spirit. "Here alone the two currents of my interest could flow together and in a united stream dig their own bed," he wrote. "Here was the empirical field common to biological and spiritual facts, which I had everywhere sought and nowhere found. Here at last was the place where the collision of nature and spirit became a reality."[1]

However, when, at the end of 1900, Jung started work as a junior psychiatrist at the Burghölzli Hospital in Zurich under Eugen Bleuler—the man who introduced the term schizophrenia into psychiatry—he discovered that his senior colleagues were less interested in the subjective meaning of their patients' distress than in classifying their symptoms, establishing a diagnosis, and compiling statistics. Since then, not an awful lot has changed. Diagnosis continues to be the primary focus of psychiatric practice, and revised editions of the *Diagnostic and Statistical Manual of Mental Disorders* are debated with a degree of hairsplitting pedantry worthy of medieval scholastics.

There have been advances, it is true. More is known about the genetics and neurophysiology of the major psychoses. Antidepressants and tranquilizers have been discovered which go some way to remove symptoms and relieve suffering. Many of the old mental hospitals have been closed down—though this achievement has proved a mixed blessing for both society and the patients. Chairs of psychiatry have been established in most universities. There has been steady progress in neuroscience, with important studies of the lateralization of function of the two cerebral hemispheres, the neural basis of memory, and the emotional implications of the limbic system. The development of brain imaging techniques using computers to construct three-dimensional images from two-dimensional data, as in computerized tomography (CT) and magnetic resonance imaging (MRI) have led to a resurrection of Kraepelin's *dementia praecox* concept of schizophrenia and have advanced our understanding of cerebral changes in conditions such as Alzheimer's disease and Korsakoff's psychosis.

Psychiatry is now, perhaps, a more respected profession than it was when Jung entered it at the beginning of the century, but not all the changes that have occurred would have met with his approval. What excited Jung about psychiatry was the intense personal engagement demanded of the doctor in the therapeutic relationship with the patient. Yet in recent years the psychiatric interview has become less personal, clinical assessment of the patient being more dependent on the use of tests, questionnaires, inventories, and team meetings than on the traditional psychiatric examination conducted in the context of the doctor-patient relationship. Moreover, because of advances in pharmacology and neurology, patients often tend to be treated as assemblies of enzymes and neuronal circuits, while their personal spiritual needs are neglected.

The Cartesian split between body and mind has been echoed throughout this century in a split between psychiatry (with its use of physical treatments) and psychotherapy (the treatment of mind by mind). Mutual hostility and misunderstanding have resulted, with the psychotherapists creaming off the rich neurotics and leaving the poor psychotics to the psychiatrists. In general psychiatry, the overall emphasis continues to be organic, behavioral, and sociological, while the psychological and spiritual aspects of mental illness receive relatively little attention.

Further advances in neurophysiology are expected to demonstrate an organic basis for the "functional" psychoses—schizophrenia and manic-depressive psychosis. While this is, of course, to be welcomed, there is grave danger that it will lead to further neglect of the spiritual needs of patients and that psychiatry will become more and more reductionist—that is to say, that it will seek to explain all the joys and sorrows, the profound insights and extraordinary inspirations of human life in the language of genetics and chemistry.

All this, Jung would have regarded as a disaster. For him,

both in his life and in his work with patients, psyche was primary, and he was convinced that no discontinuity existed between the mentally healthy and the mentally ill, that what we see in psychiatric patients is an exaggeration of processes which exist in psychiatrists themselves—who, of course, consider themselves to be normal!

In the 1970s a crisis of confidence afflicted the profession, from which it has yet to recover. Many practitioners are still demoralized by the onslaught of the anti-psychiatry movement of the 1960s, which questioned the very existence of mental illness and stigmatized psychiatrists as repressive agents of the state. The primary reason for this loss of conviction is, I believe, a fundamental failure of vision—psychiatrists generally lack a perspective wide enough to encompass the two realms of biology and psyche. Not only have psychiatrists too often failed to meet the spiritual needs of their patients, but they have also failed to establish the epistemological foundations of their discipline on the evolutionary subsoil out of which our species emerged. Intimidated by the anti-Darwinian prejudices of the behavioral scientists and fearing the contempt of their medical and surgical colleagues, psychiatrists have held onto their much hallowed medical model like shipwrecked mariners clinging to a raft.

It all looks rather depressing. Yet rescue is at hand. Although psychiatry has been in the doldrums, it could just be entering the most exciting episode in its history. The reason for this optimism is not just the evident advances in pharmacology and neuroscience, but the broader theoretical perspective being adopted by some of the brightest researchers working in the field. And to a psychiatrist steeped in the psychology of Jung, the most fascinating and promising element in these new developments is their endorsement of the central importance of the archetypal hypothesis.

I believe that a massive paradigm shift is under way, carrying us beyond the medical model with its inherent Cartesian split to an entirely new conceptual framework capable of defining the basic components of human nature, their evolutionary origins, and their essential developmental needs. Since the archetypal hypothesis gives equal weight to psychic and physical events, the new paradigm would serve to correct the materialistic and soulless biases of contemporary psychiatry. It also provides a new insight into the genesis and meaning of psychopathological phenomena. Let me explain what I mean with a parable, which, unlike most parables, happens to be true.

The Psychopathology of the Two Million-Year-Old

At the London Zoo there is a concrete mound, surrounded by a moat, known as Monkey Hill. It measures about thirty meters by eighteen. In 1925 the zoo authorities put 100 hamadryas baboons on this pitiful excrescence and expected them to settle in good-naturedly and entertain the public. They declined.

It was to have been an all-male population but, with a degree of care that proved typical of the operation, six females were accidentally included. Vicious battles for dominance took place between the males, which continued for months, and before two years had elapsed, forty-four of them were dead. But by then, a stable dominance hierarchy had been established, and an uneasy peace prevailed. However, the unfortunate creatures seemed unhappy, and in a wholly misguided attempt to cheer them up, the authorities put thirty more females on the island. Within a month, fifteen of these had been torn to pieces by the resident males fighting to possess them. By 1930, only thirty-nine males and nine females survived, and that year three males and four females were killed.[2]

What does this say about baboon psychology? Are they such

vicious brutes that they are incapable of controlling their passions and living in peace with one another? How on earth has this species survived? To answer these questions we must turn to the ethologists (those biologists who study animals living in their natural habitats), who have investigated the life of baboons in the sort of surroundings they evolved to live in. The ethologists tell us that, out of captivity, hamadryas baboons live in well-ordered social groups based on a stable dominance hierarchy; they respect each other's territories and seldom challenge heterosexual bonds once they have been formed.

Clearly, the behavior of the baboons on Monkey Hill was grossly abnormal. What went wrong? Quite simply, the circumstances in which the zoo required them to live constituted a monstrous frustration of their basic archetypal expectations. The ethogram of the hamadryas baboon—that is to say, the total archetypal endowment of the species—presupposes large areas of land on which to establish territories, win position in the social hierarchy, and, when successful in both these achievements, collect a harem of females. Instead of the 540 square meters afforded by Monkey Hill, a troop of one hundred baboons would normally require a range of 50 square kilometers—50,000 square meters—an area nearly one hundred times as great.

In normal circumstances, baboons develop intense group loyalties and are hostile to strangers from other troops. That the animals on Monkey Hill fought each other with such psychopathic savagery was due to the fact that they had been trapped and assembled from different wild troops and crowded together in a tiny area where there were more males than females and where they couldn't possibly keep out of each other's way. We must conclude, therefore, that the zoo environment in which this tragic population was placed constituted what I have called the "frustration of archetypal intent."[3] The result was gross and unmistakable psychopathology.

This sad story is an allegory of what can happen to another creature that evolved to live in the wild open spaces of the East African savanna, *Homo sapiens sapiens,* when made to live in that urban habitat which Desmond Morris called the human zoo. Directly comparable disasters to that suffered by the baboons in London Zoo occur in human communities forced to abandon their traditional way of life and live in circumstances alien to them. One such people was the Ik, a group of hunter-gatherers in Uganda who were excluded from their range of 40,000 square kilometers, placed in shack settlements, and taught subsistence farming. They rapidly became demoralized, depressed, anxious, and ill, and they behaved with psychopathic indifference to their children and their spouses.

Evidence such as this provides us with a model for psychopathology. Mental health depends upon the provision of physical and social environments capable of meeting the archetypal needs of the developing individual. Psychopathology can result when these needs are frustrated. This formulation gives rise to two fundamental questions: (1) What are the archetypal needs of the developing individual? (2) What environments, physical and social, are capable of guaranteeing their fulfillment? These, it seems to me, are the two questions that psychology and psychiatry will have to address in the twenty-first century. The myth in terms of which the answers to these questions will have to be framed is that of Darwinian biology, for the Darwinian myth is the bedrock myth of our times, and no psychological explanation can hope to survive if it is incompatible with it. When I say this, I am speaking of myth as an account of human origins that accords with the knowledge prevailing at the time of the myth's emergence into consciousness.

Every living organism has an anatomical structure and a behavioral repertoire which is uniquely adapted to the environment in which it evolved (the "environment of evolutionary adaptedness"). This is the environment in which individuals have a built-in expectation that they will live out their life cycle. Any alteration in the environment has consequences for the organism. Some changes may be compatible with survival, others may not. And changes which do not result in elimination of the species may nevertheless produce distortions in its typical modes of behavior which may lead, ultimately, to extinction.

Human versatility, coupled with a sophisticated capacity for innovation, has resulted in dramatic transformations in the environments human beings now inhabit. These environments display an astonishing diversity in comparison with the stable characteristics of the African savanna where we evolved and lived out the greatest part of our existence as hunter-gatherers. Indeed, the speed at which environments have altered in recent centuries has far outstripped the pace at which natural selection can proceed in the time-honored Darwinian manner. These considerations present problems to any researcher wishing to establish precisely what the characteristics of the environment of human adaptedness were actually like. Yet if we truly wish to understand what manner of creature we are, then the effort has to be made, for the challenges provided by our primordial environment selected the archetypal propensities still present in human beings to this day.

How can we proceed? How can we hope to establish the inventory of archetypal imperatives with which we have been equipped by evolution? One possibility is to study the lives of hunter-gatherer communities that have survived into the present century—people like the !Kung Bushmen of Botswana, so lovingly described by Laurens van der Post. But how can we know that such people were (when they were studied) as we were when we evolved? The answer is that we can't. If physical particles change their behavior when observed by physicists, then the behavior of hunter-gatherers is hardly likely to remain undisturbed when scrutinized by bespectacled anthropologists in baggy shorts. Moreover, we can't know how much modern ways had already begun to influence them before the anthropologists arrived on the scene. It is only an assumption that surviving hunter-gatherers were living closer to the original human state than populations practicing agriculture and animal husbandry. But it is, I think, a fair assumption.

What other sources of information are there? Worldwide studies of cultural universals provide invaluable data when applied in conjunction with the law I propounded earlier: that whenever a phenomenon is found to be characteristic of all human communities, irrespective of culture, race, or historical epoch, then it is an expression of an archetype of the collective unconscious.

How can we know that these consistencies are due to archetypes and not to cultural diffusion? We can't. Both factors are involved. However, there will be a bias for those characteristics which are archetypally dependent to diffuse more readily than those which are not. Whan a pattern or characteristic such as maternal bonding, dominance striving, or home building is found to satisfy three sets of criteria, it is likely to be archetypally based. These criteria are universality, continuity, and evolutionary stability.

(1) Universality: The pattern in question is found in all known cultural groups.
(2) Continuity: The record of evolution shows no sharp break between human and other mammalian species with regard to the pattern concerned. Thus attachment behavior between mothers and infants, between peers, and between mature males and females can be traced backwards from human beings through primates to their earliest mammalian origins. The major breakthrough of ethology has been to demonstrate that such patterns of behavior can be codified and their evolution studied in the same way as

the evolution of anatomical structures, such as bones, lungs, and brains.

(3) Evolutionary Stability: Patterns that are evolutionarily stable result in the same selective penalization and ultimate elimination of individuals who fail to manifest them.

Since we are a supremely social animal, the most important characteristics of the evolutionary environment for us to define are the social characteristics. In what kinds of groups did we evolve? Astonishing though it is, remarkably few anthropologists have shown any interest in establishing the basic social parameters of the environment of human adaptedness. One brave exception is Robin Fox, who has attempted to define the kind of society that is typical of hunter-gatherer communities. He refers to this society as the basic state: "Where in time is the basic state to be found?" asks Fox. "The answer is straightforward: in the Late Paleolithic, some fifteen to forty thousand years ago. It is really that simple. We were fully formed modern *Homo sapiens sapiens;* we had reached the top of the food chain—we were doing quite a bit better than the other carnivores. Then with frightening rapidity, it all began to go wrong. . . ."[4]

Fox argues that in the Upper Paleolithic a balance existed between the organism, the social system, and the environment. Then two things happened to disturb this balance: (1) the ice age, which increased the density of human populations by squeezing large numbers of peoples into southwest Europe, the Middle East, and parts of Aisa; and (2) the discovery of agriculture and animal husbandry.

The improved economy and increased numbers which these developments produced led in turn to the emergence of the characteristics typical of civilized societies—e.g., classes, castes, power elites, armies, empires, and the exploitation of subject peoples. Ever since then, "these emergent properties—seized as their subject matter by the social scientists—have been on a collision course with the social needs of the paleolithic hunter." What we call history, concludes Fox, is merely the most recent catalog of the products of this collision.[5]

Extrapolating from the extant ethnographic accounts of hunter-gatherer communities, Fox deduces that the organic groups in which our species lived for 99.5 percent of its existence consisted of about forty to fifty individuals, made up of approximately six to ten adult males, about twice that number of childbearing females, and about twenty juveniles and infants. These were "organic extended kinship groups," and they constitute what we might call the archetypal society of our kind.

Such groups did not, of course, function in isolation. They came into frequent contact with other similar groups—hence the universal human rituals of greeting, visiting, feasting, making alliances, marrying, and warring. These compact, extended kinship groups of forty to fifty members knew one another intimately and shared the same values, rules, customs, and mores, their beliefs being sustained by myth, ritual, and religion. In all of them the family was the central institution, whether polygamous, monogamous, or polyandrous.

It is in order to live in such societies as this that nature has equipped us. This is why it is that being born into the contemporary world can come as a nasty shock to the system. The archetypal endowment with which each of us is born prepares us for the natural life cycle of our species, in the natural world in which we evolved. A programmed sequence of stages, each mediated by a new set of archetypal imperatives, seeks fulfillment in the development of characteristic patterns of personality and behavior. Each set of imperatives makes its own demands on the environment. Should the environment fail to meet them, then the evident result is "the frustration of archetypal intent." For example, the infant-mother archetypal system will achieve fulfillment only if activated by the presence and behavior of a maternal figure; the paternal archetypal system can be fulfilled only by the presence of a father figure; and the heterosexual archetypal system can achieve fulfillment only through the presence of a suitable mate. Should any of these figures be absent, then the archetypal system concerned will remain dormant in the unconscious and development will be arrested or follow an aberrant course. Put in these terms, the purpose of life is the fullest possible realization of the archetypal program. Individuation is the realization of this program as consciously as possible.

We are now in a position to define a basic principle of psychopathology: Psychopathology results when the environment fails, either partially or totally, to meet one (or more) basic archetypal need(s) in the developing individual. As far as I know, the first psychiatrist to propound this principle was John Bowlby, who stated that the further the rearing environment deviates from the environment of evolutionary adaptedness, the greater the likelihood of pathological development.[6]

If we are to understand the psychiatric disorders from which our contemporaries suffer, therefore, we have to consider in what ways Western society frustrates the needs of the two million-year-old—that is to say, the primordial man or woman—within. Many possibilities immediately come to mind: the disruption of community-based kinship bonds as a result of migration, job mobility, experiments in town planning, and so on; the disruption of families through divorce and separation, together with the rapidly increasing incidence of single-parent families; the lack of adequate provision for the secure and intimate care of children whose mothers go out to work; the loss of myth, ritual, and religion; the lack of contact with nature, the seasons, and the primordial environment. All these factors are potentially productive of stress, insecurity, and anomie, as well as skewed or distorted development. It seems likely that the various neuroses, psychopathies, drug dependencies, and the occurrence of child and spouse abuse, to say nothing of the ever-rising crime statistics, are not unconnected with Western society's inability to satisfy our archetypal needs.

However, I would not wish to imply that our society is an unmitigated disaster. In fact, the contemporary environment does not differ from the archetypal environment as radically as one might imagine when it comes to meeting the basic requirements of the Self (the term Jung gave to the individuals's total archetypal endowment). For example, the physical requirements of warmth, shelter, and nourishment are met in the West better than ever before in history. The social needs for parents, peers, and potential mates are also met in the majority of individuals. However, the number of people in whom these basic needs are not met is large and growing, as indeed is the psychiatric problem which they represent.

A key factor in most psychiatric illness is stress. The probability is that the greater the gap between archetypal needs and environmental fulfillment of those needs, the greater the stress and the more incapacitating the illness. Although many people suffering from stress come to the attention of psychiatrists, many of them, perhaps the majority, do not; nor do they necessarily manifest the signs of psychiatric illness. When Jung gave up working with psychotic patients in hospitals in order to devote himself to his own research and to his private analytic practice, he noted that the people who came to consult him were not, on the whole, suffering from disorders susceptible to neat clinical diagnosis. Rather they were suffering from the aimlessness and futility of their lives. He came to regard this as a malaise typical of the twentieth century, which he called "the general neurosis of our age." Jung had no hesitation in attributing this contemporary neurosis to the emergence of social institutions that alientated us from our archetypal nature. Secular urban life breeds disalliance with the unconscious, and "disalliance with the unconscious in synonymous with loss of instinct and rootlessness."[7]

This insight has a long and respectable pedigree. In the eighteenth century, Denis Diderot maintained that the benefits of civilization had been acquired at the cost of natural happiness. The civilized person of necessity remained an unhappy creature. The theme that to be civilized we had to renounce our basic instincts was taken up by Nietzsche and developed by Freud in *Civilization and Its Discontents,* as well as by Jung in *Modern Man in Search of a Soul.* The great ethologist Konrad Lorenz compared our plight to that of a wild species that has been domesticated—like hens, cows, or hogs—living a wholly artificial existence that makes few demands of its instinctual equipment, while Desmond Morris, as we have seen, compared our lot to that of animals condemned to languish in a zoo of their own making.

Our sense of bereavement for the lost habitat of our species might explain the bouts of nostalgia which take hold from time to time for primitive life, primitive people, and primitive art—for the life of Rousseau's noble savage. It is one motive that leads many of us into a fascination with anthropology. But we should not allow it to encourage us to idealize the life of the hunter-gatherer, which, if not solitary, was often as Thomas Hobbes described it—nasty, brutish, and short!

Let me illustrate what I have been saying with an example from my own clinical experience, which shows how psychiatry and Jungian psychology can combine forces to promote insight, healing, and individuation in the face of severe frustration of archetypal intent.

"A PRETTY HOPELESS CASE"

Jennifer was twenty-one when she was sent to me by her family
doctor: "A pretty hopeless case, I'm afraid," he said in his re-
ferral letter, "but you may be able to do something for her."
Although attractive, intelligent, and well-educated, Jennifer had
never had a boyfriend or a job. She lived with her father in a
large London flat and kept house for him. Her mother had died
from injuries in a car crash when Jennifer was six. As I was
to discover at our first interview, she was a walking textbook
of psychopathology. To list only the most obvious features of
her condition, she was anxious, phobic, depressed, obsessive-
compulsive, and schizoid. I will take each of these in turn.

Anxiety: Throughout our initial interviews, she remained
tense and anxious, her skin pale and beaded with droplets of
sweat; there was a fine tremor of her hands.

Phobias: She had been a nervous child even before her
mother died, afraid of the dark, water, loud noises, animals,
strangers, and cripples. After her mother's death, she became
frightened of all novel situations. Going to school was a terrify-
ing experience, and by the time she was ten, she had developed
full-blown school phobia, with the result that her father took
her out of school and arranged private tutoring for her at home.
Although her childhood phobias had subsided by the time she
consulted me, she was nevertheless suffering from claustrophobia:
she could not use elevators or subway trains or sit comfortably
in a room unless the door was open. For the first year of her
treatment, the consulting room door had to be held open with
a volume of Jung's *Collected Works* as a doorstop.

Depression: The diagnosis of depression could be deduced
from the fact that she expressed feelings of guilt and worthlessness and wished she could summon up the courage to kill her-

self. She was disinterested in food and was as thin as a rake. She also woke early every morning in a state of dark despair.

Obsessive-compulsive neurosis: That she was obsessive was abundantly clear. She spent her life cleaning and scrubbing and was terrified that she might in some way contaminate her father's food. She was also afflicted by intrusive thoughts and images over which she could exercise no control. The most common of these were thoughts of stabbing her father and of shrieking obscenities at him. Whenever she left her apartment to do some shopping or mail a letter, she spent over an hour checking that the gas taps were turned off, all switches in the off position, all appliances unplugged, all windows shut and locked, all doors bolted and barred.

Schizoid personality: She was profoundly introverted and had withdrawn from virtually all contact with people other than her father. She compensated for this social isolation with a rich fantasy life and wrote extraordinary romantic-mythic tales, the composition of which was frequently accompanied by masturbation.

At the end of our first session I concluded that little analytic progress could be made until her symptoms had been reduced in intensity. I therefore prescribed an antidepressant and a tranquilizer and arranged to see her two hours a week for psychotherapy. The antidepressant I chose was Anafranil (clomipramine hydrochloride), a tricyclic which is particularly effective in treating depressions complicated by compulsive symptomatology. At that time the 5HT-uptake inhibitor flouxetine was not available.

When she came for her second session, she arrived four and a half hours late. What had happened was this: on her way to her first appointment with me (which, as she later confessed, she anticipated with a dread amounting to terror), she had counted the number of paces it took her to walk from her father's apartment to my consulting room. It took 2,452 paces. On her way to her second visit she knew she *had* to take *exactly* the same number of paces. She had arrived with half an hour to spare, but she had taken 2,498 paces. So she had to take a taxi home and start all over again. Next time she took 2,475 paces, so she had to go home once more. It took her four journeys to get it right, and she arrived in a state of extreme agitation.

The critical factors in her history were the early loss of her mother and the subsequent development of an exclusive relationship with her father, a brilliantly successful but emotionally unstable lawyer, who was undoubtedly devoted to her but was also tyrannically possessive and prone to unpredictable bouts of rage, as if possessed by a powerful demon. Her obsessive rituals were in part acts of propitiation to avert his fury. At the same time, her fears of killing him were a reaction formation against her own murderous feelings towards him. Her depression and sense of personal worthlessness arose because her father made her feel chronically inadequate and incapable of living up to the image of the daughter she believed he wanted her to be.

Her fear of me, and the ritual of counting the number of paces necessary to come to see me, were the result of her transferring the father imago onto me as well as the archetype of the shaman, the medicine man, the healer.[8] The counting ritual had to be gone through as a means of propitiating me and guaranteeing that I would not become incensed with her in the course of her session. The door had to be left open for the same reason: it would guarantee a hurried exit should the demon become operative in me.

For her subsequent appointments I gave her an hour late in the day so that she would be able to sort out her counting rituals and get to my door in time. She got quite good at this after a while, though she often had to hop the last twenty or thirty paces, much to the entertainment of passers by.

After she had been on Anafranil three weeks, her depression began to lift, and a week later she was able to come to see me by taxi, thus avoiding the need to count her steps. At this point, a conventional psychiatrist would probably have reduced her sessions to once a month. I, on the other hand, increased them to three times a week. With the subsidence of her more incapacitating symptoms, the analysis could begin.

What archetypal imperatives had been frustrated in Jennifer's personal history? The age of six is far too early for any child to lose its mother with impunity. This tragedy not only deprived Jennifer of the rich nourishment of a mother's love, but of a female role model to initiate her into womanhood. It also left her with an unresolved Electra complex and an inability to relate to any man except her father.

The absence of an extended family network further emphasized her exclusive dependency on her father. She had a grandmother surviving in southern Ireland, an aunt in northern Scotland, a cousin in Los Angeles, and another in Perth, western Australia. She had no friends or acquaintances in London. There was, you could say without any fear of contradiction, a lack of kinship libido and community feeling in her life. The absence of siblings and peers during childhood had contributed to her schizoid withdrawal, having deprived her of the opportunity which both peer bonding and play bring to the development of emotional spontaneity and the skills of social intercourse. Moreover, she had no contact with animals (her father would not allow them on account of the mess), with nature (she seldom left London), or with religion (her father was an atheist). Her only pleasures were her fantasy life and music (she was a good pianist, and her father had a large record collection).

As a result of these frustrations of archetypal intent, her

development had gone seriously awry. The loss of her mother not only predisposed her to depression and impaired her development of what Erik Erikson calls identity formation but effectively imprisoned her in the father-daughter relationship.[9]

Why should her symptoms have become particularly bad as she entered her twenties? Well, this is the archetypal stage of courtship, marriage, achieving social position, and, in the modern world, getting a job. None of these had she achieved or even attempted, but the pressure of the Self towards realization of all this potential was increasing, and something had to give. The result was the emergence of this formidable array of symptomatology.

THE PSYCHOBIOLOGY OF SYMPTOMS

What can psychobiology tell us about the nature of her symptoms? How can we relate them to the two million-year-old woman in Jennifer's psyche? Let us turn to each symptom again.

Anxiety: In the course of the present century the idea has been current that anxiety is neurotic and that the well-adjusted person would never suffer from it. This, of course, is nonsense. Anxiety is a natural and universal experience, which human beings share with all mammals. Since it is ubiquitous, it must serve a biological function, otherwise it would not have evolved or at least not have persisted. What then are the biological functions of anxiety?

Anxiety is a form of vigilance. To survive in this dangerous world, an organism has to be alert to environmental changes so that it can be prepared to meet whatever emergencies may arise. Pavlov considered this vigilance to be a reflex, and he called it the "What is it?" reflex. Vigilance or the "What is it?" reflex does not necessarily give rise to anxiety. Vigilance is merely alertness to the possibility of change in the environment. Vigilance shifts into anxiety when a possible threat or danger has been perceived. The actual experience of anxiety is directly associated with physiological changes that prepare the body for violent action. The heart rate increases, the blood pressure goes up, adrenaline is secreted, energy stores are mobilized in the liver and released into the bloodstream, blood is redistributed from the internal organs so as to carry oxygen and energy to the muscles and the brain. At the same time, the thyroid gland is stimulated to increase the efficiency of body metabolism. Labored breathing occurs, and the large muscles used in violent action are brought to peak efficiency. Red corpuscles are liberated from the spleen to increase the oxygen-carrying capacity of the blood. Small muscles at the base of the hair follicles contract causing goose pimples to form and the hair to stand on end, the sweat glands secrete profusely, and so on. All these changes are caused by activation of the sympathetic nervous system and have the effect of preparing the organism to fight like a demon or run like hell—the fight or flight response.

In the environment of evolutionary adaptedness, therefore, vigilance and anxiety are crucial to survival. In the modern world, however, they can seem exaggerated or inappropriate. When anxiety is exaggerated, inappropriate, and persistent, it becomes a symptom of interest to psychiatrists—and to the pharmaceutical industry (and its shareholders). A crucial question for psychopathology is why a natural psychophysiological response (anxiety) should become exaggerated into a persistent and inappropriate neurotic state (anxiety neurosis).

There have been a number of theoretical approaches to this question. The most influential of these has been the Freudian approach, which sees neuroses as the direct result of traumatic experiences in early childhood. This was certainly true in Jennifer's case. Life cruelly deprived her of a mother long before she was able to survive happily without one, and life failed to provide her with peers at the time when she needed them.

The consequences of separation from or loss of mother have received particular attention from the British analysts Bowlby, Fairbairn, and Winnicott.[10] Bowlby, in particular, was careful to base his work in ethology, and for this reason his formulations will guide us for many years to come. Throughout Bowlby's work one fundamental notion persists—the idea that noncorrespondence between the developing needs of the child and conditions prevailing in its environment contributes to its susceptibility to neurosis. I once gave a paper in London comparing Bowlby's approach with Jung's when Bowlby was present. In discussion afterwards he agreed that he accepted the Jungian formulation that neurosis is liable to occur when the archetypal program unfolding in the psyche of the child is not met by correspondingly appropriate figures and situations in the environment. Essentially, he was in agreement with the proposition that neurotic anxiety results from the frustration of archetypal intent. And this, in my view, rather than any specific trauma suffered in infancy, is the cause of psychiatric disturbance in childhood, adolescence, and later life.

Phobia: Psychiatry makes a distinction between free-floating anxiety, which may be evoked by a variety of different situations, and phobic anxiety, which is specific to one situation, such as confined spaces, open spaces with no cover, snakes, spiders, predatory beasts, strangers, heights, and so on. It is of the utmost interest for our theme that when the various phobias suffered by modern men and women are examined in detail, there is nothing modern about them. They are all exaggerated fears of objects, animals, or situations that were potentially life-threatening in the environment of evolutionary adaptedness.

This vital point is invariably overlooked in textbooks of psychiatry, probably because it is not apparent until you think about it. Conditions that give rise to flight, withdrawal, or other demonstrations of fear, both in animals and in humans, are not necessarily dangerous in themselves; but when you consider them carefully, it becomes clear that they are related, if only indirectly, to situations that actually are a hazard to life or limb. As Bowlby put it:

> In a wide array of animal species including man, a principal condition that elicits alarm and retreat is mere strangeness. Others are noise, and objects that rapidly expand or approach; and also, for animals of some species though not for others, darkness. Yet another is isolation.
>
> Now it is obvious that none of these stimulus situations is in itself dangerous. Yet, when looked at through evolutionary spectacles, their role in promoting survival is not difficult to see. Noise, strangeness, rapid approach, isolation, and for many species darkness too — all are conditions statistically associated with an increased risk of danger.[11]

The tendency to react with fear to such common stimulus situations is due to genetic biases that possess survival value, in the sense that they prepare individuals to meet real dangers. The existence of these biases would explain how it is that in modern civilized environments fear can be aroused in a variety of situations that are not, in fact, dangerous. Thus, to show panic fear in response to finding oneself in an enclosed space like an elevator or a subway train, to react with terror in response to the perception of height or the realization that one is entirely alone in the dark may seem absurd to a normally adjusted person, but viewed from a biological standpoint, these reactions are understandable as manifestations of ancient response patterns. What the individual is responding to are the natural cues, or sign stimuli, commonly associated with danger in the environment of evolutionary adaptedness. Often these cues do not signify any menace, but the fact remains that they *could*.

Therefore, it is not altogether inappropriate for the individual to respond to them with wariness or fear, if only on the principle that it is better to be safe than sorry.

Now the form of phobia selected by the patient is usually full of symbolic meaning. You will recall that Jennifer's phobia was of confined spaces. Claustrophobia is evidently an exaggeration of the natural response shared by all mammals to being trapped in an enclosed area and deprived of all means of escape. It is not surprising, therefore, that it is found in clinical practice that claustrophobia commonly occurs in people who experience home as suffocating and parents as oppressors. Whereas agoraphobics experience the outside world as threatening and feel secure only at home, for claustrophobics it is home that arouses anxiety, and there is a desire to flee from the threatening enclosure that home represents. Characteristically, the claustrophobic flees not only from physical enclosure but imprisonment in social roles from which there is no means of escape. As a result, commitments such as marriage and a job are far too dangerous to be risked. This was precisely Jennifer's condition when she entered analysis.

Depression: People who are prone to depression are typically those who have experienced some form of parental loss, rejection, or neglect in childhood. Depressive illness tends to recur when the individual suffers some new frustration of his or her archetypal needs: this new frustration is experienced as a recapitulation of the original depressing or frustrating experience of childhood. Analysis reveals the nature of the original frustrating experience and points to the kind of analytic work that needs to be done during the rest of therapy.

As with anxiety, depression is also a natural and universal experience human beings share with all mammalian species. It thus must be a biological condition contributing to survival. What can its function be? On the whole it appears that depression is an adaptive reaction to loss or deprivation. It occurs, for example, in all young mammals when they are forcibly separated from their mothers and in all individuals living in hierarchically organized groups when deprived of rank in the social hierarchy. How can this contribute to survival? Having lost its mother, and after the initial cries of protest are over, the depressed infant lies still, silent and waiting, conserves body energy, and avoids the attention of predators. By this strategy the animal can survive until reunited with its mother or adopted by a surrogate parent, moved by its depressed state. Similarly, a depressive reaction to loss of status enables the demoted individual to adapt passively to the lower rank, thus avoiding further attack from the more powerful individual who has displaced him or her. This in turn contributes to peace and social cohesion.[12] Depression, therefore, is linked with the ubiquitous mammalian tactic of submission, while its opposite, mania, is linked with the tactic of dominance. Manic-depression is thus inextricably tied into the dominance-submission archetypal system and its linked systems, aggression and defense. In Jennifer's case, her depression was linked to her submission to her father's dominance and to her perceived inability to make her way in the world.

Obsessive-compulsive neurosis: Obsessive-compulsive behavior is a by-product of the need to control potentially dangerous events, objects, people, thoughts, feelings, impulses, or situations. It is commonly associated with powerful emotions, particularly fear, anger, and guilt. Guilt, like anxiety, depression, and anger, is an emotion to which all social animals are prone. It evolved as an adaptive device designed to maintain social order and homogeneity. Like anxiety, it can be exaggerated and become the symptom of neurotic illness. This occurs most markedly in the case of obsessive neurosis. Exaggerated guilt and obsessive-compulsive behavior are more likely to occur in homes ruled by the principle of Logos and least likely in those ruled by Eros.

Guilt is evoked by thoughts, feelings, and actions that offend against whatever moral authority the individual was brought up to respect and which became internalized in the form of the moral complex, that inner patriarch or matriarch which Freud called the superego. Guilt and obsessive-compulsive neurosis are more apparent in people who have internalized their authorities out of fear rather than out of love. Typically, those who have been brought up through fear bear a grudge against authority and wish to defy it, however much they may overtly subscribe to its values. As a result, a conflict rages in them between the desire for defiance and the need to submit. Locked in this conflict, the patient feels compelled to think or do things that are foreign to his or her conscious personality. In this manner, Jennifer was obsessed by thoughts of murdering her father and felt compelled to engage in all manner of rituals to prevent these thoughts from achieving their objective. Moreover, her condition largely owed its origins and its severity to the fact that her father was himself an obsessive-compulsive personality.

Because of a constant terror that things may get out of hand, obsessive individuals are driven by a compulsion to control events and people. What is intolerable is anything spontaneous, fortuitous, or unpredictable. In his book *Anxiety and Neurosis,* Charles Rycroft describes the attitude obsessives adopt to their own emotional life and that of people around them as reminiscent of a colonial governor ruling an alien and potentially rebellious population, or like an animal in possession of a territory over which it has established absolute power and mastery. They treat all spontaneous tendencies, all uncensored emotions, as if they were dangerous invaders. That is to say, they go on the attack either to expel intruders or to force them into submission.

When the intruder is an alienated part of the Self, the attack is recognized by analysts as repression. This formulation helps us to understand why it is that the shadow is particularly threatening to the obsessive person. The shadow has to be ruthlessly beaten into submission for fear that it might otherwise get out of control. This single fact presented me with the most formidable obstacle to a successful outcome in Jennifer's case. I do not believe I could have succeeded were it not for the pharmacological assistance provided by Anafranil.

Schizoid personality: It is often asserted that schizoid personalities do not become depressed; they are too detached, it is thought, to be depressive. In fact, I have known a number of schizoid people who suffered from depression, and I take this, when it happens, as a positive prognostic sign — that they are not so detached from reality as to be unconcerned about what is happening in their lives. This was certainly true in Jennifer's case.

Why do people become schizoid? In part, it is a response to disappointment of basic social needs, but it can also be related to an innate introversion. Schizoid people typically had parents who were either absent for critical periods in their childhood or showed little regard for them as people in their own right. Such parents seem to overlook the fact that their children have thoughts and feelings of their own; they tend to treat them like dolls to be picked up, put down, packed off to school, or put away in a nursery, as seems most convenient. As a consequence, the child grows up distrusting all human relationships, feeling that its own needs and wishes will never be considered. In these circumstances, the most practical strategy is to opt out from people and retreat into oneself. The schizoid withdrawal from social life into a self-absorbed introversion is thus an appropriate response to repeated frustration of those archetypal imperatives concerned with social development. This is what had happened to Jennifer.

Shut up in the isolated citadel of the self, what happens

to the archetypes of the collective unconscious? They may remain latent as unconscious potential, they may manifest in dreams and fantasies, or they may be experienced as threatening symptoms—things to be feared and if possible controlled, denied, or repressed. The latter course is the most dangerous, as the repressed archetypal components are projected out onto figures in the environment, and "that way madness lies." At the beginning of her treatment, I was alarmed to discover that this had begun to occur to Jennifer, and it got into the transference. She reacted with paranoid sensitivity to my most innocent remarks, and there were occasions when she couldn't bear for me to look at her. Just as her claustrophobia prevented her from traveling in subway trains, so her paranoid sensitivity prevented her from riding on buses. She felt people were looking at her, commenting on her, and laughing at her.

This exquisite self-consciousness is common to both schizoid personalities and schizophrenics. The fear of being looked at or stared at is the fear of having one's defenses penetrated, of being evicted from one's inner citadel. The eye is one of the most common features of schizotypal art. How are we to relate this phenomenon to our evolutionary heritage? Ethological studies have shown that staring and visual attention are very important in all social mammals. The higher a dominant animal ranks in the social hierarchy, the more the less-dominant members of the society stare and attend to that one's needs. The dominant animal accepts such attention as rightfully due and is unperturbed by it, but if a subdominant animal is stared at by a dominant animal, the subdominant experiences it as frightening and intimidating. A dominant animal's stare is usually one of reproof and is aggressive in intent.[13]

The same is true in human communities. Kings, queens, presidents, prime ministers, television personalities, and pop stars all thrive on being looked at and attended to. Their self-esteem usually glories in such scrutiny. But a person of low status who is stared at, or one with feelings of low self-esteem, experiences it as threatening and a cause for alarm. For this reason, for a schizoid or schizophrenic patient, whose self-esteem is almost invariably impaired, dislike of being stared at is a normal mammalian response.

A further archetypal component of staring is that of the predator. Predators stare unblinkingly and with intense fascination at their prey. Men waiting in ambush to attack potential victims behave in precisely the same way. Staring is a primordial feature of the enemy archetype. There are, therefore, biological analogues for anxiety about being looked at, being distinctive, or drawing attention to oneself. Camouflage is, after all, a defense mechanism apparent throughout nature. Vulnerable individuals defend themselves from attack by merging with the landscape and rendering themselves inconspicuous. This is at the bottom of all fears of being different.

The schizoid phenomenon is one that we can readily understand because there is a sense in which any reasonably well educated person in our culture can also be said to be schizoid. The scientific disciplines that have emerged in the last three hundred years teach us to separate ourselves from the outer world in order to look at it objectively and dispassionately. Indeed the philosopher whose insights made the scientific method possible was himself a schizoid personality.[14] René Descartes taught us to depersonalize the world and to separate our minds from our bodies. Before that, we probably tended to personalize the world of things and to read human intentions into all existence, as children continue to do to this day, until adults educate it out of them.

In dealing with schizoid patients, the crucial questions are (1) how far has retreat into the citadel proceeded? and (2) to what extent has the ego succeeded in both sustaining some kind of relationship to outer reality and at the same time entering into a creative relationship with the Self? Fortunately, in Jennifer's case, she had not retreated so far as to preclude the forming of a therapeutic relationship. Moreover, her rich fantasy life meant that she was in creative relationship with the Self, and I was able to mobilize this in the service of the analysis. It was not an easy ride. No sooner did she begin to trust me than she entered a phase of intense anxious attachment to me. She often experienced difficulty in leaving at the end of sessions. I had to cope with suicide threats on weekends and holidays, and she concocted a series of rituals to go through each time she left my consulting room to ensure that I would still be well disposed to her when she returned on the next occasion.

What was my duty as her doctor-analyst? Essentially, I conceived these to be as follows: (1) to render her symptoms less incapacitating; (2) to become the good father who wanted her to grow up and take on the tasks of adulthood; (3) to mobilize the individuation principle in the Self; and (4) to encourage her to leave home, get a job, become independent of her father, and begin to stand on her own feet. Finally when these goals had been achieved, I regarded it as essential to refer her to a woman analyst, who could help her to affirm her identity with the feminine principle and to experience herself as a woman.

And was this ambitious therapeutic program achieved? To a greater or lesser extent, I am relieved to report, it was. It was three years before she was able to leave her father, set up house on her own, and find a job as a receptionist in a doctor's clinic. A year later, I referred her to a woman analyst, and a year after that she married a publisher. All that was a long time ago. But when I contacted her recently to request her permission to use her history, suitably disguised, she seemed well and happy. She has two adolescent children, works for an animal welfare agency, is a vegetarian and a Buddhist, and she is still with the man she married fifteen years ago—no mean feat these days.

In the name of clinical honesty I must declare, however, that the successful outcome of this case depended as much on the use of Anafranil as on the analysis. Obsessive-compulsive patients are the hardest to analyze, especially when they are depressed or have a schizoid personality. Without pharmacological help the analysis might have been stillborn, because we would probably have remained bogged down in her appalling symptoms. But if, on the other hand, I had merely played the role of a psychiatrist and contented myself with removing her symptoms, she would in all probability still be stuck at home with her aged father, and her individuation would be no further along.

I have discussed this case at such length because it illustrates how the frustration of archetypal intentions can result in severe psychopathology and how the use of conventional psychiatric assessment and treatment may be combined with Jungian analysis to facilitate healing.

THE FIVE LAWS OF PSYCHODYNAMICS

We are now in a position to propose five laws of psychodynamics:

> *First Law:* Whenever a phenomenon is found to be characteristic of all human communities, irrespective of culture, race, or historical epoch, then it is an expression of an archetype of the collective unconscious.
>
> *Second Law:* Archetypes possess an inherent dynamic, whose goal is to actualize themselves in both psyche and behavior.
>
> *Third Law:* Mental health results from the fulfillment of archetypal goals.
>
> *Fourth Law:* Psychopathology results from the frustration of archetypal goals.

Fifth Law: Psychiatric symptoms are persistent exaggerations
of natural psychophysiological responses.

These laws, which appear to us to be explicitly about human psychic functioning, are in fact mere applications to the
psyche of laws whose operation is apparent throughout nature.
Thus, the acorn will become the best oak tree it can, given the
nature of the soil, the condition of the climate, the proximity
and height of the surrounding trees, and so on. Deficiencies
in any of these environmental conditions will result in stunting
or susceptibility to disease, such as dieback, the mystery disease
afflicting many oak trees in Britain at the present time.

It is important to recognize that the frustration of archetypal
intent can occur at any stage of the life cycle, and not only in
childhood as Freud supposed. For this reason, Jung did not consider that psychopathology is invariably related to earlier traumatic childhood experience. Unlike Freud, Jung recognized that
development proceeds throughout the *whole* life cycle, and that
every stage has its own archetypal goals. The truth of this view
has been confirmed empirically. George Brown and his colleagues
have shown from studies based on their Social Research Unit
in London that individuals who can depend on the physical and
verbal expression of attachment from an intimate companion
enjoy a vital social asset protecting them from depression and
neurotic distress. They found that it was not at all uncommon
for anxiety and depression to be caused, not by childhood deprivation, but by a major life event which revealed that current
personal relationships were unsupportive and uncaring.[15]

The fifth law—that psychiatric symptoms are persistent exaggerations of natural psychophysiological responses—was not
only proposed by Freud and by Jung but has been reaffirmed
by the contemporary ethopsychiatrists. For example, Brant
Wenegrat of the Stanford University Medical Center in Califor-

nia sees all psychopathological syndromes, whether psychotic, neurotic, or psychopathic, as statistically abnormal manifestations of innate response strategies shared by *all* individuals, whether they are mentally healthy or ill. As we saw earlier, by innate response strategies, Wenegrat means the same as archetypes. Wenegrat's understanding of psychopathology is in complete agreement with Jung's position. As Jung wrote: "We have known for a long time that the mentality of the neurotic is basically normal, though marred on the surface by exaggeration and disproportion. In other words, the neurotic is normal apart from certain anomalies. . . ."[16]

Jung maintained that the same could be said of the psychotic: "Nothing produced by the human mind is completely outside our psychic range. Even the craziest idea must derive from something within the human mind, from some hidden root or premise. Without definitive evidence to the contrary, we cannot suppose certain minds to contain elements that other minds do not contain at all. . . ." He concluded that insanity "is merely the manifestation of a hidden, yet generally existent, condition." It is as if the dreaming mode persists in the waking brain, and for this reason the psychotic lives in closer relationship with the two million-year-old through a form of *participation mystique*. In psychosis, the "Number One" personality ceases to be effective, and the "Number Two" takes over. Adaptation to the outer world is consequently defective.[17]

THE CRUCIAL ARCHETYPAL SYSTEMS

Of the archetypal systems studied by the new breed of biologically oriented psychiatrists — the ethopsychiatrists — that concerned with care giving has certainly received the closest attention. But one other system is beginning to achieve almost as much importance — that concerned with competition.

In a major work, *Human Nature and Suffering,* Paul Gilbert describes four distinct biosocial goals which he sees as fundamental. These are care giving and care receiving (the archetypal systems studied by Bowlby) and competing and cooperating (the archetypal systems at the heart of Alfred Adler's work). Success in pursuit of these goals, according to Gilbert, results in both psychiatric health and genetic fitness (that is to say, the individual is more likely to pass his or her genes on to the next generation). Failure in pursuit of these goals, on the other hand, results in psychopathology.

Care provision is a cornerstone of human culture and there is a good biological reason for this — not only is a caring community better able to succeed in the struggle for survival, but, in the modern biological view, our genes see to it that we care for others who carry similar genes to our own. What matters in nature is not primarily that individuals should reproduce themselves, but that their genes should survive. The most efficient way of achieving this is through progeny, but it can also be achieved by assisting kin (who inevitably carry a proportion of the same genes). This is the post-Darwinian idea that natural selection operates not on individuals but on genes. The notion of *inclusive* reproductive fitness has come to replace Darwin's theory of *sexual* reproductive fitness. Thus, behavior like altruism has been selected and plays an important part in the life of all social mammals. Why should this be? Why should I put my life at risk to protect my children, siblings, or cousins? The answer is that as far as nature is concerned the survival of one's genes is every bit as important as, if not more important than, the survival of one's clan. Altruism, nurturance, and care giving are thus genetically transmitted response strategies, to use the sociobiological term adopted by Wenegrat, which function at the core of human nature.

Yet, as a society, the most telling accusation that can be

made is that we are not very good at caring for each other, and our failure in this regard lies at the root of so many of our human miseries. The great lack in urban life, as we saw in Jennifer's case, is the lack of kinship libido. Perhaps those of us who are drawn into the caring professions are driven by a collective *enantiodromia* — a compensatory attempt to make good what has been lost. The cold, classical Freudian approach failed to provide this. Gilbert suggests that the reason why Kohut's self psychology has been so popular and has had such a powerful influence on psychoanalytic theory is because it has provided a therapeutic rationale for therapists to be warm, accepting, and involved with their patients — something that Jung was advocating long ago.

However, as Friedrich Nietzsche and Alfred Adler observed, we are not just nurturant, caring creatures; we are aggressive, acquisitive, and status hungry as well. This description applies not only to the emotionally frustrated — it is true of humanity as whole.

There are, it seems, two types of hunter-gatherer societies:[18]

Type One: The simplest type of society is based on an economy of immediate consumption, and there are no obvious hierarchies, though the personal dominance of some individuals is evident.

Type Two: The more sophisticated type of society is one in which surpluses of food and resources are accumulated, and these societies show the beginnings of clear social rank.

In all primate societies, sexual selection has ensured that males of high rank reproduce more than males of low rank. The resulting inequality (or social asymmetry) is maintained by force — not by the police, but by the occurrence of tournaments known by the ethologists as ritual agonistic behavior. Success in status conflict (dominance) is associated, as we have already seen, with elation (mania), and failure (submission) with despondency (depression).

Thus, like all other primates — and all other mammals for that matter — we are both affiliative and hostile, we want both attachments and status, we are both Freudian and Adlerian or, in Aristotle's terms, both hedonic and political. This basic dichotomy has been studied by Michael Chance of the Social Systems Institute in Birmingham. Chance describes two different and antithetical types of social systems operating in primate societies (including our own), which he designates the hedonic and agonic modes respectively. The hedonic mode is characteristic of affiliative groups, in which the members offer mutual support. The agonic mode is characteristic of hierarchically organized groups, where members are concerned with their status and with warding off threats to it.[19]

In the agonic mode tension, arousal, and stress are at a high level; in the hedonic mode things are infinitely more relaxed. There is an evident link here with the mobilized and relaxed states described by Anthony Wallace, and which I have described as typical of human populations in times of war and in times of peace.[20]

The distinctions Chance makes between two fundamental social modes are in line with similar distinctions occurring in the history of ideas. There are parallels, for example, with Freud's Eros and Thanatos instincts: Eros, the life instinct, expresses itself in the act of bonding, integrating, and creating; Thanatos, the death instinct, in dissolving, disintegrating, and destroying. Freud hardly used the term Thanatos in his published work, perferring the terms "destructive instinct" and, occasionally, "instinct to mastery" or "will to power."

Moreover, in Freud's theoretical division of the instincts we find echoes of the antithesis made by Empedocles between the two great opposing but equal principles presiding over the perpetual fluxes of all existence, which he called love and strife. Freud acknowledged this connection. "The two fundamental principles of Empedocles—love and strife—are," wrote Freud, "both in name and function, the same as our own two primal instincts *Eros* and *destructiveness* [Thanatos]."[21]

Many other similar parallels could be drawn—as, for example, the valuable distinction made by Gordon Rattray Taylor between egalitarian, affiliative *matrist* societies and authoritarian, aggressive *patrist* societies, the distinction made by classical Chinese philosophy between Yin and Yang, Jung's distinction between Eros and Logos principles, and so on.[22] For convenience, these parallels are summarized in Table 1.

Table 1.
Parallel Dichotomies

Chinese	Yin	Yang
Aristotle	hedonic life	political life
Empedocles	love	strife
Ethology	bonding and attachment	ritual agonistic behavior
Gilbert	care giving and care receiving	cooperating and competing
Chance	hedonic mode	agonic mode
Wallace	relaxed state	mobilized state
Taylor	matrist society	patrist society
Freud	Eros instinct	Thanatos instinct
Jung	Eros principle	Logos principle

In short, the evidence points to the existence of two great archetypal systems: (1) that concerned with attachment, affiliation, care giving, care receiving, and altruism; and (2) that concerned with rank, status, discipline, law and order, territory, and possessions. These are, it seems, the basic archetypal patterns on which health and sickness depend. Both function healthily when evoked in appropriate circumstances, but either can give rise to pathology when their goals are frustrated or when they are inappropriately activated.

For example, when relations between husbands and wives or between parents and children go wrong, it is because they have shifted from the hedonic to the agonic mode. Expressions of love, nurturance, and support give way to expressions of anger, disappointment, and resentment. Status attacking and efforts to dominate and control take the place of caresses and loving styles of relating. When a decisive and lasting shift from the hedonic to the agonic mode occurs within either the family structure or the personality structure of the individual members of the family, the way is prepared for physical abuse, sexual abuse, substance abuse, and identity abuse. All of these are likely to coincide with a rising incidence of anxiety, emotional stress, depression, alcoholism, crime and suicide, to help inflate the psychiatirc statistics.[23] These disasters are examples of individuation being shunted onto the wrong track.

The two social archetypal systems, corresponding to Aristotle's hedonic and political levels of life, should not so dazzle us with their significance that we overlook his third level, which was of such crucial importance to Jung: the contemplative life. For this represents the activity of a third great archetypal imperative — that concerned with the perception of meaning. As Jung said at the end of his BBC interview with John Freeman, human beings "cannot live a meaningless life."

HEALING

As we saw in the case of Jennifer, the approaches of conventional psychiatry and Jungian psychology can assist one another in achieving a satisfactory therapeutic outcome, especially when the illness is understood as having a biological basis and as representing a frustrated attempt at individuation.

Jung has often been criticized for his failure to make a clear distinction between normal and abnormal psychology and for not developing a coherent theory of neurosis, psychosis, or psychopathy. This was in part a revolt against Freud's reductionism but also, more significantly, a reflection of his belief that mental health and mental illness are both expressions of the soul's quest for growth and meaning. Jung sought to transcend the distinctions so beloved of clinical psychiatrists by taking the psyche as primary and developing techniques to further its quest for individuation. Psychiatric diagnoses then became of less critical importance.

"Hidden in the neurosis is a bit of still undeveloped personality," wrote Jung, "a precious fragment of the psyche, lacking which a man is condemned to resignation, bitterness, and everything else that is hostile to life." He goes on, "A neurosis is by no means merely a negative thing, it is also something positive."[24] In other words, the illness is symptomatic of the psyche's effort to heal itself. It is the healing wound.

For psychotherapy to have a successful outcome, it is essential for the therapeutic relationship to function in the hedonic mode. Therapies that stress the importance of negative transference, rage, aggression, jealousy, and hostility, and which give little space for expressions of affection, nurturance, and attachment, are, in my view, destructive. In good therapy, the agonistic must be contained within the hedonic rather than the other way around.

The course of healing proceeds autonomously. To succeed, the healer—whether psychiatrist, psychotherapist, shaman, or medicine man—must act in such a way as to flow with the healing intention of the Self. "A man is ill," wrote Jung, "but the illness is Nature's attempt to heal him." And again, "In the neurosis is hidden one's worst enemy and best friend."[25] The neurosis also acts as a noxious stimulus, which goads the individual to seek help. When Jung observed of a patient "Thank God he became neurotic," he meant that thanks to the neurosis the patient had been shaken out of his apathy and his resistance to change.

Neurosis and certain forms of psychosis can, therefore, be understood as the consequences of vigilance and as extensions of anxiety, fear, and paranoia—biological functions that alert us to danger or potential injury and motivate us to circumvent it. Our contemporary mental illnesses are not only persistent exaggerations of ancient responses: they also represent a desperate attempt on the part of the two million-year-old human being to adjust to the contemporary world.

4.

The Therapeutic Quest

*An analyst can help his patient just as far as he himself has gone
and not a step further.*
—C. G. JUNG, *Collected Works,* vol. 16

*The object of therapy is not the neurosis but the person
who has the neurosis.*
—C. G. JUNG, *Collected Works,* vol. 10

IN RECENT DECADES we have witnessed a phenomenon I would
never have thought likely when I entered medical school in
1956. In those days we accepted without question the idea that
all forms of illness would ultimately be defeated by the trium-
phant progress of medical science. But nowadays we have to
modify that view. Although new discoveries have continued to
be made, new drugs introduced, and new surgical techniques
developed, there has, at the same time, been a remarkable re-
naissance of "alternative" therapeutic traditions, such as chiropractic, acupuncture, herbalism, yoga, aromatherapy, and so on,
which orthodox medicine regards as hopelessly unscientific and
therapeutically useless—the esoteric refuge of the ignorant, the
credulous, and the half-baked.

Why should millions of our contemporaries display disen-
chantment with the wonders of modern medicine on such a
scale? Clearly, for all its technological miracles, orthodox medi-

cine is failing to provide its patients, or its potential patients, with what they require. How are we to understand this fascinating phenomenon? The growth of alternative therapies, despite the advances and the opposition of orthodox medicine, is a direct consequence of an archetypal predisposition in the two million-year-old within us to seek out forms of treatment that have always been "known" (gnosis) to be healing. This archetypal need lies at the heart of the therapeutic quest.

Conventional doctors are seen as deficient when they fail to meet this need—when their clinical detachment and their emphasis on technology leave the two million-year-old feeling unconsidered, abandoned, and bereft. How is this sad failure to be rectified? It will not be, I believe, until we understand that the doctor-patient relationship is an archetypal relationship, which has been with us since the beginning of time. If the goal of the therapeutic quest is to be achieved, it will not be solely through faith in scientific progress but also through a journey around that mysterious kingdom where the archetypal healer reigns eternally as monarch.

There are two avenues of approach to this awesome power: the outer (anthropological) one and the inner (psychological). By using these two approaches, we shall attempt to discover what it is that the two million-year-old patient is questing for and what it is in practice that he or she usually gets.

THE ANTHROPOLOGICAL APPROACH

When feeling under the weather, what does the two million-year-old seek? What have human beings always done when disturbed or disorientated, frightened or depressed, in pain or sick at heart? Presumably, like all other primates, they have sought comfort from their kin. But what if the suffering is greater than kin can assuage? Here anthropology indicates that "professional" assistance is sought from the medicine man or woman, shaman, witch doctor, priest, or healer.

It must be remembered that we evolved in circumstances of great vulnerability, threatened by the elements, by predators, by hostile neighbors, and by malevolent influences bringing disease and death. It is not surprising that in such conditions a figure emerged possessing great power and importance. That figure was the healer, whose role was crucial in all cultures, whose status was invariably higher—usually much higher—than that enjoyed by physicians or priests in our own society. The healer's ubiquitous power and influence reflect a demand for healing as old as our species, and the associated beliefs, rituals, and practices are among the most striking of all cultural universals.

One thing is certain, therefore: healing is based on an archetype. This is a crucial point, because the archetypal view reveals that healing is not just a matter of diagnosis and treatment; it is a question of channeling powerful propensities that are as old as evolution itself. Indeed, we can see it as being a manifestation of a cosmic healing force at work. Evolution occurs when a dysfunctional gap existing between an organism and its environment is remedied by a genetic mutation that closes the gap and results in better adjustment or adaptation.

Nature can thus be conceived as a great self-correcting process. Jung saw this self-correcting process as achieving its highest manifestation in the workings of the human psyche. Healing—particularly psychic healing, and perhaps all forms of healing necessarily involve the psyche—is the art of providing optimum circumstances in which the self-correcting powers of nature can most efficiently achieve their purpose.

The healer is one who perceives what is needed and knows how to alter the circumstances so as to make it possible for the organism to heal itself. In other words, healing is an act of enablement. Although it is seldom acknowledged, the most advanced therapeutic interventions of medical science are as dependent on these self-healing propensities as are the ministrations of traditional shamans. Hence the old saying, "God heals, and the physician takes the fee."

However, the attitude of Western doctors to traditional healers has, with a few honorable exceptions, displayed a mixture of patronizing condescension and ill-disguised contempt. Given the great advances of medical science, this view is perhaps forgivable when taken by physicians or surgeons, but much less so when adopted by psychiatrists, whose success in treating mental patients is not noticeably greater than that of their traditional colleagues. In fact, studies in Nigeria have revealed that when two groups of mental patients are treated differently — one by Western methods and the other by traditional methods — patients treated by the witch doctor do considerably better.[1]

This is not the place to develop a critique of Western psychiatric practice, but it can be argued with some justice that in our society mental patients receive something less than optimal care. Frequently voiced criticisms, especially by patients, are that psychiatrists do not take enough time to listen, that they tend to treat symptoms rather than people, and that they lay more emphasis on the use of drugs and social manipulation than on the one-to-one healer-sufferer relationship. We can add to this indictment the neglect of both the spiritual and archetypal dimensions, the failure to address the meaning and purpose of the illness and to understand the transformative potential of "breakdown" in terms of the patient's individuation, the rejection of the placebo effect (thus prohibiting the use of a powerful therapeutic tool), and so on.

When they are called upon to give an account of the achievements of their specialty in this century, psychiatrists invariably talk about the introduction of phenothiazine drugs and of their "integrated programs" for pharmacological, psychological, and social treatment and rehabilitation, as if these were startlingly innovative and new. In fact, Indian Ayurvedic medicine has used a powerful drug in the successful treatment of psychotic disorders for thousands of years. This drug, *Rauwolfia serpentina*, was first introduced into Western medicine in 1954 but has been superseded by chlorpromazine, which is not more effective but is thought to have less depressing side effects. Rauwolfia has also been used by traditional healers in Africa—though it is not known for how long, since no written records exist.[2]

Moreover, the use of occupational therapy and progressive programs of social and vocational rehabilitation are nothing new. Similar policies were advocated by William Tuke early in the nineteenth century at the York Retreat, at Gheel in Holland in the seventeenth century, and by traditional healers for no one knows how many centuries before that. One Kenyan healer reported that most of his psychotic patients worked for him: "After a week some recover, then I do not let them stay idle. They cultivate, fetch water, I send them to market and to the flour mill, and they cut grass in the compound." He said he was careful to assess each patient's capacity for work and allocated only a job of which he or she was capable.[3]

All this should give us cause for reflection. The truth is that we are so far from being triumphantly aware of what goes on in a successful encounter between therapist and patient that we are in no position to look down our noses at traditional healers and their practices. Instead of despising them, we would do better to examine the possibility that they may have something to teach us. After all, the techniques of primitive healing are the primordial roots from which medicine, psychiatry, *and* psychotheraphy have all grown. Although I have no personal experience of traditional healers, I have long been fascinated by ethnographic accounts of their work. Reading about them, I am overwhelmed by feelings of awe and humility when I compare their life with my own. The most impressive thing about them is the degree of individuation required to accomplish the tasks expected of them.

Healers have always had to do more than look after the health and welfare of their people. They were the ones you went to if you needed rain or victory in war. They knew all about the gods and goddesses and the ancestral spirits; they could tell you how the world began and sing you all the historic deeds of the tribe. They could also create spells against enemies and provide protection from hostile sorcery. Evidently, what made them effective as healers was not just their learning but also their charisma and status. As one authority has commented: "In the presence of a disease, especially a severe or dangerous one, the patient places his confidence and hopes in the *person* of the healer rather than his medications. . . . It would therefore seem that the healer's personality is the principle agent in the cure, in addition to any skill or knowledge."[4]

On the whole, the ethnographic evidence would suggest that the two million-year-old patient looks to the healer for four things: (1) *authority* or charisma; (2) personal *attention* — to be given time to be heard and understood; (3) *knowledge* — a corpus of theory and practice from which the healer can provide a diagnosis, an explanation, and an appropriate treatment; and (4) *restoration to health* and full participation in the community.

Three basic types of healer have been described: *noninspirational* or lay healers treat with "rational" methods, such as fasting, massage, or herbs; *inspirational* healers or magicians undergo ritual possession (a variety of self-hypnosis similar to the self-induced trance of Western mediums) and treat through suggestion, using their prestige; *priests* or *shamans* may undergo a severe mental disturbance, rather like a psychosis or Jung's "confrontation with the unconscious" after his break with Freud (this may be regarded as an "initiatory illness" or what Ellenberger calls a creative illness). Before we consider the various theories of healing to which these different types of healers subscribe, we must first turn to the inner (psychological) approach to the healer archetype.

THE PSYCHOLOGICAL APPROACH

Healing is the central mystery of analysis. All analysts, like all doctors of whatever kind, even the least competent of them, have experienced the wonder of seeing patients, who came to them in distress, get better. We are often tempted to think this is because of our own expert ministrations, but in our hearts we know it is because of something that happens beyond our reach and usually beyond our comprehension. It happens somewhere in the patient and somehow in the alchemy of the analytic relationship.

It also happens somewhere in the analyst. At the most telling moment in an analytic session, it is the healer who intervenes and inspires the analyst's words. When we are young and freshly qualified, the ego wants to blurt out clever things it has read in a book or heard in a lecture, but that is seldom very helpful. With time, the ego acquires a little humility. It learns to sit quietly and wait for the healer to gather its intuitions and speak. The experienced analyst knows that the healing spirit is present in the analytic *temenos* and that it has to be somehow contacted and evoked. The ego then becomes the executive through whom the healer operates, the channel through which healing flows.

In an effort to understand the relationship between the Western doctor and the archetypal healer, I have attempted to examine what goes on in myself. The first thing to say is that the doctor in me is mostly ego. He proceeds consciously and logically—at least as consciously and logically as he is able. He takes a history, he does an examination, he makes a diagnosis, he works out the pathology, and he draws up a plan of treatment. The healer, on the other hand, is altogether more unconscious. Sometimes he is accessible and sometimes he is not.

Confronted with a disturbed patient in the clinical situation, the doctor in me is sometimes stymied. Faced with the patient's demands on me, the doctor hasn't much idea what he ought to say. The healer, on the other hand, is seldom stymied. He is more imaginative, far more inventive. That is why, I believe, the art of healing depends on the constellation of the healer in the self. We have to cultivate him, circumambulate him, relate to him, lend him our vocal chords, and let him speak.

In my own experience, the most productive interventions of the analyst come straight out of the unconscious. Faced with the patient's suffering, I am stirred emphatically. That is the beginning. Wounds open, and we both suffer the pain. Nothing more may happen. But on occasion, and without warning, an intuition rumbles somewhere beneath the ego's feet: an insight erupts and I find myself giving voice. There is then a moment of electricity. Something changes in the total situation. When it's all over, I think, Now what on earth was *that!*

This is not a rare or unprecedented phenomenon. Not even the least conscious, most completely unanalyzed doctor can escape the archetypal field in which the healer operates. For the doctor-patient relationship is itself an archetypal system with two poles, between which energy, symbolism, and physical interaction flow. The doctor-patient transaction is like any other archetypal relationship which is constellated between two people, each holding the opposite pole of the other—the parent-child, teacher-pupil, husband-wife, leader-follower, and so on.

The essence of the doctor-patient archetypal system is beautifully expressed in the ancient symbol of the wounded healer. The Greek god of healing, Asklepios, was himself taught the art of healing by Chiron, a centaur. And Chiron suffered from an incurable wound. A slightly later version of the wounded healer is seen is the crucified Christ.[5] As with all archetypal symbols, the wounded healer finds the widest possible expression. In ancient Egypt, for example, the dog goddess Labartu was the goddess of healing. But she had two names: in addition to Labartu she was known as Gula, and as Gula she was the goddess of death. The Hindu goddess Kali was held responsible for the pox, but she was also indispensable for its cure. The Greek god Apollo, who could cure plagues, also caused them.

This brings us closer to the central mystery of healing. The archetypal image of the wounded healer makes comprehensible how it is that doctor and patient are related not only externally but internally as well.[6] In every doctor there is a patient, and in every patient a healer. What draws most of us into the profession of healing, I suspect, is the sick patient in ourselves questing for its other half for completion. It is, if you like, our mode of individuation. As therapists, consciousness of our wound and our personal therapeutic quest is a primary duty. Hence the training analysis we all go through. Our wound is our personal equation.

All archetypal relationships are acted out in childhood play. Play is nature's high school. It is a preparation for living out the relationship in adult life. It is no mere coincidence that playing doctors and patients is part of the childhood experience of most of us. Indeed, some of us get so fixated in the game that we go on playing it for the rest of our lives.

One reason why so many people prefer to consult alternative practitioners rather than physicians and psychiatrists is that modern doctors split the archetype of the wounded healer into its two poles, identifying themselves exclusively with the healer and projecting their wounds into their patients. In this way, doctors bask in the illusion that they are entirely healthy while their patients are entirely sick. Now this has unfortunate consequences, particularly in the practice of psychiatry. By disallowing their own woundedness and projecting it wholly into their patients, psychiatrists add to the severity of their patients' wounds. For their part, the patients are encouraged to renounce the healer at work within themselves and to project it instead onto the person of the doctor, thus adding to the doctor's power and self-satisfaction.

This is not to say, of course, that doctors should refuse to receive the projection of the healer from patients. What I am saying is that doctors need to be aware of their own woundedness if they are to empathize with their patient's inner plight. This facilitates the later withdrawal of the healer projection so that patients can learn to cooperate with the healer at work within themselves, thus becoming less dependent on doctors. As all archetypes do once they have been activated, the healer *personates* in the personal psyche—sometimes as a man, sometimes as a woman, and sometimes as a bear, dog, serpent, or other animal or object, like the mandala, possessing healing power. The healer appears in dreams and in active imagination and is felt as a numinous presence in the transference and countertransference, as well as in the healing doctor-patient relationship.

Freud introduced the term transference to describe the unconscious process by which patients attribute to their analysts qualities that were, in fact, possessed by significant people in their own past and relate to the analyst as if he or she were one of those figures. Since the most common imagos to be projected onto the analyst are the mother and father, the healer is frequently experienced as a parental figure. Jung discovered that much more was involved in the transference than this, however. Archetypes are stirred up by the analytic relationship. When projected onto the person of the analyst, these archetypes confer great therapeutic — or great destructive — power. In Jung's experience, the archetypes most commonly projected onto him were the magician, shaman, witch doctor, quack, charlatan, savior, alchemist, and wise old man. The activation of these archetypal figures seems to be crucial to the healing process, and it would explain why it is that the authority, the charisma, the degree of individuation attained by healers is so important for their success. As Jung observed, you cannot hope to take people further than you have gone yourself.

Let us now look at the various modes of healing which prevailed in the world up to the present time.

The Principles and Practices of Healing

Enough parallels can be drawn from the mass of data relating to the activities of traditional medicine men and women to demonstrate a fair measure of agreement ranging across many different cultures and over an enormous geographical spread. These parallels reveal a broad consensus on the major theories of disease causation and the principles of treatment on which medical practice has been traditionally based.

At the risk of being accused of outrageous simplification, I maintain that these can be subsumed under two basic theories of pathology: (1) something has got out of the patient which *ought* to be there, and (2) something has got into the patient which ought *not* be there. Each of these theories is linked with its own appropriate principle of treatment. If something has got out, replace it. If something has got in, remove it. We will examine each of these in turn.

Something has got out. One of the oldest explanatory theories of the phenomena of life and death makes use of the idea that each of us possesses a ghostly entity, which in our culture we call the soul. This entity, it is believed, enters us at birth, or at conception, or while we are in the womb and has the capacity to leave our bodies in certain critical circumstances. The moment of death is an obvious example. Many peoples accept this phenomenon as the explanation of dreams — namely, that our souls actually go off and do the things we dream about while we are asleep. Many also accept it as an explanation of one category of disease, described as loss of soul.

There are different theoretical explanations as to how the soul can come to be lost, but most are agreed that the night is a particularly perilous time. One might, for example, be waked up suddenly from a dream while one's soul is wandering in a far-off place, so that its passage of return is forgotten. Or the traveling soul might be captured by evil spirits. Successful treatment depends on locating the soul and returning it to its rightful owner. This usually means bargaining with the spirit hijackers and paying them some form of ransom. Or it may mean a terrible struggle with them to wrest the soul free. Shamans are particularly skilled in these heroic feats.

Clinical descriptions of persons considered to be suffering from loss of soul reveal a condition closely akin to what we call depression. For example, in Peru the Quechua Indians recognize a condition they call *Michko*. People afflicted with this disease are physically and mentally retarded, lose weight and energy, display considerable irritability, and suffer from insomnia and nightmares.[7]

Western parallels to the notion of loss of soul range from the departure and return of the anima spirit in the *mortificatio* of alchemy to the bereavement which follows the loss of someone beloved. Above all, the clinical condition of depression is experienced as one in which something indispensable is missing, while recovery is experienced as the return of the vital spark of life. When depressed, one feels estranged and alienated from self and others. Treating patients in this condition, the analyst becomes the carrier of the soul and the healing energy of the psyche until such time as the patient can take them back.

In *Modern Man in Search of a Soul* Jung diagnosed our whole culture as suffering from loss of soul. He cured the condition in himself through his confrontation with the unconscious, a shamanic initiation which gave us the whole corpus of theory, practice, and technique that we call analytical psychology. However, this discipline clearly has roots which go back much further than to Zurich or Vienna at the beginning of this century.

Something has got in. In many traditional cultures illness is regarded as a manifestation of the archetype of the evil intruder—that is to say, it is thought to be an external force or object which has intruded into the body. Such an alien force or object is not merely the cause of the illness: it *is* the illness. Healing consists of removing it.

Among the Nepalese, for example, the healer sucks the illness from the patient and spits out what on subsequent examination proves to be a piece of animal or vegetable tissue onto a brass plate. This he hands round to the assembled company, graciously acknowledging their applause.[8] In the Philippines, so-called psychic surgeons carry out "operations" without the use of instruments. With their bare hands they knead the abdomen of patients and remove tissues which have the appearance of bloody internal organs. However, when the "extracted" tissues are analyzed, they again prove to be of animal origin.[9]

We cannot escape the conclusion, therefore, that traditional healers are not above the use of bare-faced trickery. And not only do they get away with it, but it works. Charlatanism heals! How can this be? As Jung once observed with that famous twinkle in his eye: *Mundus vult dicipi*—the world wants to be deceived.

Evidently the object extracted by the healer serves as a *symbol* of the disease. It is what Winnicott would have called a transitional object.[10] The secret of healers lies in the power of their personality and actions to excite in patients the belief that their disease has been accurately diagnosed and cured. Healers convince them that they are no longer ill but well. This is what hypnosis achieves, and it explains why so many traditional healers make use of trance. The patients' conviction that they are being cured is also, of course, at the bottom of the placebo effect.

Much modern practice is no less predicated on the notion that something has got in that ought to be got out—infecting organisms, foreign bodies, poisons, cholesterol, and so on. Modern surgeons are not above removing parts of their patients on the presumption that they might be responsible for making them ill, either now or in the future. How many people are needlessly deprived each year of their appendices, tonsils, uteri, and foreskins! Modern patients love to display their gallstones, kidney stones, and extracted teeth, demonstrating to themselves and to their unfortunate visitors that the cause of their illness has been removed and placed outside their bodies. This is also at the basis of much successful art therapy and the psychotherapeutic procedures of abreaction, psychodrama, and "writing things down." Patients put their inner disturbances outside themselves and are relieved in the process. Verbal communication of their inner troubles to a friend or therapist has much the same effect. Healing by exteriorization, the release of pus (emotional or physical) to the outside, is a healing procedure as old as time.

One greatly dreaded force widely believed to have the capacity for "getting in" and causing disease, especially mental disease, is the force of evil. Psychiatric textbooks describe the history of mental illness as one of linear progress from theories of demonic possession, through the Enlightenment view of madness as illness, up to the present apotheosis of neuropsychiatry and the dopamine hypothesis. We should not be taken in by this highly suspect version of psychiatric history. By replacing demonic theories with neuroscientific theories, much practical progress has been made, but in the process we have devalued the spirit and lost touch with the meanings enshrined in the old therapeutic rituals and myths. A new history of psychiatry needs to be written, which would do justice to the total human condition, giving attention to what we have lost as well as to what we have gained.

The theory of "possession," with its treatment by exorcism, is the rhizome from which dynamic psychiatry and analysis have sprouted: from Father Gassner's public exorcism of hysterical nuns in 1775, Anton Mesmer's stunning therapeutic successes in Vienna and Paris in the 1780s, and Justinus Kerner's treatment of the Seeress of Prevorst and the immensely successful book he wrote about it, to Charcot's dramatic induction and removal of hysterical paralysis at the Salpetrière and Breuer and Freud's cure of Anna O. through the talking treatment. All this grew out of the ancient theory and practice of possession and exorcism.

Moreover, the notion that psychiatric illness is caused by evil spirits which must be exorcised still unconsciously influences modern psychiatrists in what they say and do. To psychiatrists, mental illness is an enemy onto which they project their shadow—their own unacknowledged illness and evil. They conceive mental illness as something to be fought and overcome. In this sense the modern psychiatrist is clearly heir to the exorcist. Projecting the devil into the illness, the psychiatrist uses pills and electric shocks to exorcise the patient and drive the devil out.

The idea that illness is due to possession by evil spirits also goes along with the parallel concept of illness as due to sin — namely, that the patient has brought on the illness through evil-doing. The healer treats these conditions by hearing the patient's confession, granting absolution, and performing rituals for the propitiation of the gods.

Modern psychiatry, like analysis, has replaced the idea of "sin" with the notion of "guilt." There is little doubt that confession in the consulting room plays a fundamental role in psychotherapeutic success. Patients often feel they are unworthy to be members of the human race, that they are beyond the pale. Modern therapists, no less than ancient healers, can restore patients to the bosom of the human family through their healing ministrations.

Theories of evil, witchcraft, and sorcery play a large part in traditional concepts of disease, particularly in countries like Ghana where paranoid ideas are prevalent. Ghanaian houses, trucks, canoes, and workers' toolboxes are decorated with such legends as "Trust no man," "Enemies everywhere around me," "Fear men and play with snakes." One authority tells the story of a Ghanaian carpenter who got some grit in his eye while riding his bicycle. He made no attempt to have the particle removed but rushed off to a diviner to find out who had put it there.[11]

Jungian analysts understand paranoid ideas as resulting from shadow projection onto an out-group, which is then perceived as hostile. Patients are encouraged to become conscious of their shadow, to assume personal responsibility for it, and to stop projecting it out onto others. With paranoid schizophrenics, however, this can prove a tough proposition. Here I draw on the wisdom of the traditional witch doctor and employ counter-magic. I offer it in the form of a potion—in this case a phenothiazine pill.

In our culture the archetype of the healer is embodied in the figure of Jesus Christ. "And his fame went throughout all Syria: and they brought unto Him all sick people that were taken with diverse diseases and torments, and those which were possessed with devils, and those which were lunatic, and those that had the palsy; and He healed them" (Matthew 4:23–24).

As Julian Leff points out in his invaluable *Psychiatry around the Globe,* Jesus' healing technique was similar to that used by native healers throughout the world when dealing with mental illness. The healer commands the devil to leave the possessed sufferer, transfers the evil spirit to the bodies of animals, and the animals are subsequently killed. There is the additional element of water, which is used to wash away the spirits. St. Mark tells us of one psychotic, a vagrant of no fixed abode who lived among tombs, who approached Jesus and asked him for help. When Jesus asked his name, he gave the moving reply, "My name is Legion, for we are so many." The account goes on: "Now there was there nigh unto the mountains a great herd of swine feeding. And all the devils besought him, saying, Send us into the swine, that we may enter into them. And forthwith Jesus gave them leave. And the unclean spirits went out, and entered the swine: and the herd ran violently down a steep place into the sea (they were about two thousand;) and were choked in the sea" (Mark 5:11–13).

Numerous parallels to this can be found in the ethnographic literature. For example, Yoruba healers stand their mental patients in a swiftly flowing river. They use three doves as living sponges to wash the evil away from the patient. The doves are then killed and their bodies flung downstream, and the evil is carried away by the river.[12] Such measures in indigenous practice are usually effective, as they were in Jesus' treatment of Legion. And they still are effective—in the natural world of dreams. Those of us who practice as Jungian analysts are not, of course, in the habit of commanding spirits into animals and taking them to the sea or to a river to be drowned. But such symbolism is found again and again in the dreams and fantasies of our patients. It is our task to enable the patient to participate as fully as possible in the psychic drama as it is played out. In this we perform the same role as traditional healers.

ATTAINING THE GOAL

Healers have always understood the importance of ritual. In ancient Greece, for example, there were more than three hundred sanctuaries dedicated to Asklepios. These were places of great beauty, surrounded by hills, woods, and sacred streams, in close proximity to the sea. To get to an Asklepion required a long, hazardous journey by ship and donkey. When you arrived, you underwent ritual purification. Your clothing was removed, you drank and bathed in the sacred waters, and then you put on clean clothing. At the altar you made sacrifice and paid homage to Asklepios. Then you were led into the *abaton,* the sacred abode of the god. There a sleeping draught was administered, and you were left to sleep — on the ground in earliest times (*incubation* means lying on the ground) but later on a couch, called the *kline* (the forerunner of the Freudian analytic couch and the examination table in the doctor's clinic). You then went to sleep and Asklepios or his symbolic representative, the serpent, which bit the afflicted part, invariably appeared to you in a dream, conveying a message of healing that could itself be instrumental in producing a cure. The dream required no interpretation: the experience was itself the cure.

The influence of Asklepios began to decline after the time of Hippocrates, who died in Larissa in 356 B.C. at the astonishing age (if the scribes are to be believed) of 104. Hippocrates is celebrated by medical historians for his — I quote — "forthright rejection of the magic and sorcery of the priest-healers of the Asklepian cult," and for his emphasis on observation, rational diagnosis, and established remedies.[13] It is tempting to see this moment in history as the origin of the conflict between ortho-dox medical science and alternative therapeutic traditions. But I suspect that the conflict is much older than this. It is an ex-pression of our ancient archetypal propensity for polarizing issues and taking sides. Ultimately, such conflicts are a function of the evolutionary history of the human psyche and are related to the fundamental structure of the human brain. With our modern understanding of cerebral lateralization and the differ-ent functions of the two sides of the brain, we can see that in being more rational, and eschewing magic and the use of rit-ual, therapeutic medicine has become increasingly dominated by the thinking function and has become the preserve of the left cerebral hemisphere with its sequential, verbal, digital modes of functioning. Modern physicians and psychiatrists are the heirs of Hippocrates, while "alternative" therapists and analysts are the heirs of Asklepios, upholders of the feeling, symbolic, and intuitive functions, operating more in the realm of the right cerebral hemisphere (holistic, nonverbal, and analogical) and the limbic system of the old mammalian brain (and its archetypal modes of response).

In my view, both approaches have their place, and each is impoverished if deprived of the other. Alfred J. Ziegler has re-ferred to these two therapeutic approaches as sanistic (from the Latin *sanitas,* meaning health, *sanus,* meaning healthy, and *sanare,* to make healthy) for the Hippocratic, left-brained approach, and morbistic (relating directly to the "morbid" quality of disease) for the Asklepian, right-brained mode. They can also be de-scribed as allopathic and homeopathic, respectively. Sanistic therapies are full of solar symbolism, and the gods who rule over them are sun gods—Apollo, Heracles, and Helios. The sym-bolism of the morbistic approach, on the other hand, is any-thing but solar. On the contrary, it is underworldly.[14]

In Greek mythology, the most heroic deed of Apollo was

to overcome a being who was his absolute "other," the monstrous Python, which inhabited the swamp near Delphi and threatened to destroy all humanity. This symbolizes the apotheosis of the dominant left hemisphere and its triumph over the world through the use of reason, discipline, and self-control.

The relationship between Apollo and the Python can be traced in the fourfold evolutionary structure of our brains shown in figure 2.

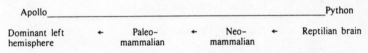

Figure 2. The Evolutionary Structure of the Brain

Earlier I mentioned Paul MacLean's concept of the triune brain (see figure 1, p. 22)—the idea that the human brain is not, as was previously thought, a single organ but three brains in one, each representing a stage in evolutionary development, and each with its own intelligence, memory, and patterns of behavior. Los Angeles neuroscientist Jim Henry has argued that the dominant hemisphere represents a fourth and most recent cerebral development, which is peculiar to our species.[15]

In Jungian terms, sanistic therapies mobilize the energies of the conscious ego while morbistic therapies are designed to mobilize those of the Self. These parallels and associations are summarized in Table 2.

Morbistic therapy is, in Ziegler's phrase, "empathy-based therapy." Instead of fighting or suppressing the illness, one goes down into it, taking it on as "a legitimate part of the order of things."[16] In contrast to the sanistic, left-hemispheric approach of post-Hippocratic medical science, analysis is inclined more

Table 2.
The Psyche and Its Therapeutic Quest

Left (dominant) hemisphere	Right hemisphere and limbic system
Orthodox medicine	Alternative medicine
Hippocrates	Asklepios
Sanistic (allopathic) therapies	Morbistic (homeopathic) therapies
Apollo	The Python
Psychiatry	Analysis
Ego	The Self

The Transcendent Function

The Corpus Callosum

to the underworldly, morbistic approach of the Asklepian alternative. Analysis is empathy-based — as are homeopathy and shamanism. Through the training analysis, the analyst learns what it is to be in the patient's place and to live in intimate relationship to the morbid. However, analysis does not favor Python at the expense of Apollo: it gives due weight to both sides of the struggle. The rituals of analysis are designed to stimulate the healing powers residing in the natural world of the dreamer, a world which, shaman-like, analysts know at first hand through their daily work with the unconscious in their patients and in themselves. The paleolithic underworld is a resource forever imminently present, but Apollonian clarity is not to be sacrificed to the Stygian depths. Dialogue is the way — between upper and lower, inner and outer, linking the contemporary with the archetypal world.

To Jung, mental illness resulted from a loss of contact between the subjective and objective psyches, between conscious and unconscious personalities, between the ego and the Self. The way to healing was to bring the two sides together — in other words, to activate that psychic function which he called transcendent. The transcendent function represents the unconscious will to health; it is the principle of individuation in action, an expression of the profound human longing to evolve toward a higher level of personal integration and consciousness. As Ernest Rossi has suggested, the aim of Jungian analysis may be understood in neurological terms as the attempt to promote bilateral hemispheric integration through increasing communication in both directions across the corpus callosum (the great bundle of fibers connecting both sides of the brain).[17]

Let me illustrate what I mean with another dream involving a sword. This sword was very old and richly ornamented. In the dream it was dug up from a tumulus and presented to the dreamer, an unmarried woman who was in analysis with Jung. When asked for her associations, she recalled an image of her father holding a dagger, which flashed brilliantly in the sunlight. Her father was an energetic, strong-willed man who had had numerous love affairs and had died when the dreamer was still very young. She had, nevertheless, formed a strong father complex, though she tended to become involved with men who were weak and neurotic and very much unlike him.

Now if Freud had been analyzing this woman, he would have seen the sword as a phallic symbol and would have concluded that her preference for weak men was due to the repression of her incestuous desire for her father. Jung, however, went an important step further. When she entered analysis, the patient herself had been weak and neurotic. Through the image of the sword, her unconscious was telling her that she could be strong and healthy like her father. In other words, Jung's interpretation was offering her a way out of her illness, a course for future action. The sword represented her will to health. It was *phallos* (in Monick's terms), a sacred generative power like Osiris's Djed, restored by Isis, the ultimate goddess figure, representing the feminine soul.[18] It was a symbol embodying the transcendent function.

In recent decades there have been numerous attempts to assess the effectiveness of different forms of psychotherapy, and there seems to be fairly general agreement that, contrary to the assertions of the Freudians, insight and analysis of the transference are not indispensable to favorable outcome. It is claimed that certain basic characteristics are present in all psychotherapies, including psychoanalysis—the prestige and genuineness of the therapist, the positive relationship established with the patient, a shared world view, a belief on the part of the patient that the procedure will prove helpful, and so on. All these enhance the main therapeutic influence, namely, *suggestion*.[19]

Now I would not wish to deny the importance of suggestion. But I believe it is important only because of its influence on more fundamental forces. I refer to the endogenous powers of healing present in the patient. Psychotherapy, autogenic training, hypnosis, meditation, divine healing, relaxation techniques, the placebo response, and a whole host of "alternative" techniques work—when they *do* work—because they succeed in activating these endogenous powers.

Jungian theory sees itself as going one stage further than this. Indeed, its course can be understood as one long process of mobilizing the transcendent function, using dreams and active imagination to grant the ego access to the archetypal world within. The relationship between these two realms of experience is represented by the belief of many West African peoples in a prenatal contract made by each individual with a heavenly double. According to this West African view, before you enter the world, you draw up a contract with your double as to what you will do in the course of your life—how long you will live, what your life's work will be, how you will serve your community, whom you will marry, how many children you will have, and so on. Then, just before you are born, you are led to the Tree of Forgetfulness, which you embrace, and from that moment you lose all conscious recollection of your contract. However, you must nevertheless live up to all your contractual undertakings. If you do not, you will become ill, and you will need the help of a diviner, who will use all his skill to make contact with your heavenly double and discover what articles of the contract you are violating or failing to fulfill.[20] In our Western society, the role of the diviner is taken over by the Jungian analyst.

By attending to the paleolithic inner world, we can not only further our personal individuation but make our own contribution to redressing the gross imbalances of our culture. Can we do any more than this on the political, social, or ecological front? This, it seems to me, is the crucial question of our time, and it is far too enormous to be answered here. But we can at least frame it in the terms we have been using. If many of our psychic ills are due to the frustration of archetypal intentions by the circumstances in which we now live, what may we do about making the two million-year-old man or woman within us feel more at home in the contemporary world?

We can drastically reduce the world's population over the course of the next two centuries; reverse the rabid destruction of natural habitats and the ecosystem; reestablish the centers of human life in small, mutually supportive communities; promote a reverential attitude to all creation; allow a new mythic or religious orientation to emerge enabling us to see ourselves as the servants of nature rather than the masters. The list is endless.

There is no knowing how any of this may be achieved, but if the Self wills it, it must be achievable. To gain access to the archetypal world, to begin to know the unknowable, is at least a beginning. The natural world of our planet now depends for its whole future survival on what it can achieve through its intrapsychic representative — the primordial survivor in ourselves.

Epilogue

THE HISTORY OF DREAM PSYCHOLOGY has been rife with conflict between those who see dreams as communications rich with significance and those who see them as meaningless waste products of brain physiology. As Freud wrote at the end of the last century: "Dreaming has often been compared with the 'ten fingers of a man, who knows nothing of music, wandering over the keys of a piano' . . . and this simile shows as well as anything the sort of opinion that is usually held of dreaming by representatives of the exact sciences. On this view a dream is something wholly and completely incapable of interpretation; for how could the ten fingers of an unmusical player produce a piece of music?"[1]

This attitude persists in the analogies so beloved of contemporary dream scientists like Crick and Mitchison, who compare dreaming to the clearing out of redundant information from a computer. This hypothesis, which has received so much attention in learned journals, is nothing new. It was proposed in the 1880s by Robert, who described dreams as "a somatic process of excretion." "A man deprived of the capacity of dreaming," Robert wrote, "would in course of time become mentally deranged, because a great mass of uncompleted, unworked-out thoughts and superficial impressions would accumulate in his brain and would be bound by their bulk to smother the thoughts that should be assimilated into his memory as completed wholes." Summing up Robert's position, Freud characterized dreams as "scavengers of the mind."[2] We might describe this as the theory of the dream as phagocyte (phagocytes are those scavenging white corpuscles which remove toxic substances from the blood). When we read these authors, it is hard to escape the fantasy that they have all been influenced by *The Doctor's Dilemma,* the play in which George Bernard Shaw memorably described all professions as "conspiracies against the laity" and had a medical fanatic declare, "There is at bottom only one genuinely scientific treatment for all diseases, and that is to stimulate the phagocytes." When it comes to the scientific treatment of all dreams, many contemporary researchers seem to be of the same opinion.

While I have no wish to escape the demands of scientific method, I would nevertheless advocate a holistic approach to the dream — something which the scientists, through their dedication to theoretical parsimony and experimental rigor, often fail to do. It does not seem to me unreasonable to propose that the hermeneutic (interpretative) and the scientific (experimental) approaches to the dream should complement and correct one another to their mutual advantage.

The fact is that dream scientists and neurophysiologists have added greatly to our comprehension of the dream. If they are to be criticized, it is for the persistent reductionism of their approach. The danger is that the more we think of ourselves as computers the more we shall become like them. It is important to stress this point so that we do not languish into the apathy of the Elgonyi medicine man who lamented to Jung his people's loss of their dreams. Rather, we should regard dreams as an endangered species, as Liam Hudson has suggested, a potential casualty of technological advance.[3] To prevent this, we must continue to place great value on our dreams. They should be respected as feral, in the sense of Robert Bly's wild man, and we must resist all attempts to "scientize" them.

As we wander ever further into the materialist desert that our civilization has become, our dreams are the only oases of spiritual vitality left to us. They represent our primordial habitat, our last wilderness, and we must protect them with as much fervor as the rain forests, the ozone layer, the elephant, and the whale.

In the meantime, the primordial survivor continues to speak to us in our dreams with the voice and spirit of Osiris. We should not encourage Set to dismember him. But when, inevitably, he does, we must never fail to summon Isis to aid us in reassembling the parts and reuniting them into a whole—including not just the Freudian phallus, but the sacred and generative *phallos*.

Notes

PROLOGUE

1. James Hillman. *The Dream and the Underworld*, p. 6.
2. C. G. Jung, *The Collected Works*, vol. 8, para. 420.
3. Jung, *Collected Works*, vol. 18, para. 1228.

CHAPTER 1: KNOWING THE UNKNOWABLE

1. C. G. Jung, *Memories, Dreams, Reflections*, p. 297.
2. Ibid., p. 53.
3. Jung, *Collected Works*, vol. 5, para. 259, and vol. 8, para. 339.
4. John Locke, *Essay Concerning Human Understanding*, Book II, emphasis in original.
5. W. H. Auden, *A Certain World*, p. 33.
6. Jung, *Collected Works*, vol. 8, para. 420; C. G. Jung and W. Pauli, *The Interpretation and Nature of the Psyche*.
7. Jung, *Collected Works*, vol. 8, para. 450, emphasis added.
8. Victor Turner, "Body, Brain, and Culture," *Zygon* 18 (Sept., 1983): 221–45.
9. George P. Murdock, "The Common Denominator of Culture," in *The Science of Man in the World Culture*, ed. R. Linton; Robin Fox, *Encounter with Anthropology*.
10. Jung, *Collected Works*, vol. 11, para. 146.
11. Klaus-Peter Koepping, *Adolf Bastian and the Psychic Unity of Mankind*.

12. Claude Lévi-Strauss, *Structural Anthropology*, pp. 18, 22; Eugene d'Aquili, "The Influence of Jung on the Works of Lévi-Strauss," *Journal of the History of Behavioural Science* 11 (1975); Paul Kugler, *The Alchemy of Discourse: An Archetypal Approach to Language.*

13. Claude Lévi-Strauss, *The Savage Mind*, p. 65; Jung, *Collected Works*, vol. 9(1), para. 155.

14. Kugler, *Alchemy of Discourse*, p. 46.

15. Fox, *The Search for Society*, pp. 19, 20, 34.

16. Niko Tinbergen, *The Study of Instinct.*

17. Jung, *Collected Works*, vol. 18, para. 1228.

18. Charles J. Lumsden and Edward O. Wilson, *Promethean Fire: Reflections on the Origins of Mind*; C. H. Waddington, *The Strategy of the Genes: A Discussion of Some Aspects of Theoretical Biology*, p. 79.

19. Paul D. MacLean. *The Triune Concept of the Brain and Behaviour.*

20. Eugene Aserinsky and Nathaniel Kleitman, "Regularly Occurring Periods of Eye Motility and Concurrent Phenomena during Sleep," *Science* 118 (1953): 273–74; Michel Jouvet, "The Function of Dreaming: A Neurophysiologist's Point of View," in *Handbook of Psychobiology*, ed. M. S. Gazzaniga and C. Blakemore.

21. Brant Wenegrat, *Sociobiology and Mental Disorder*; Russell Gardner, "Psychiatric Syndromes as Infrastructure for Intra-specific Communication," and John Price, "Alternative Channels for Negotiating Asymmetry in Social Relationships," both in *Social Fabrics of the Mind*, ed. M. R. A. Chance; Paul Gilbert, *Human Nature and Suffering*; Anthony Stevens, *Archetypes: A Natural History of the Self.*

22. Noam Chomsky, *Aspects of the Theory of Syntax.*

23. Nancy Burson, "Androgyne" (composite photograph), *Harper's*, June, 1985, p. 28.

24. Kugler, *Alchemy of Discourse.*

25. Jung, *Memories, Dreams, Reflections*, pp. 245–46.

26. Ibid., p. 244.

27. Ibid., p. 231.

28. Ibid., p. 239.

29. Ibid., p. 247.

30. Paul J. Stern, *The Haunted Prophet*, p. 172.

31. Jung, *Collected Works*, vol. 10, para. 978.

Chapter 2: Dreaming Myths

1. Carl Sagan, *The Dragons of Eden*.

2. Calvin S. Hall and Vernon J. Nordby, *The Individual and His Dreams*, p. 19, emphasis in original.

3. Ibid., pp. 33, 35.

4. Ibid., p. 11.

5. Ibid., p. 26.

6. Richard Griffith, O. Miyagi, and A. Tago, "The Universality of Typical Dreams: Japanese versus Americans." *American Anthropologist* 60 (1958): 1173-78.

7. Jung, *Collected Works*, vol. 11, para. 146.

8. J. Allan Hobson, *The Dreaming Brain*, p. 294.

9. Ibid.

10. Jung, *Collected Works*, vol. 16, para. 351.

11. C. G. Jung, *Psychological Reflections: A New Anthology of His Writings, 1905-1961*, p. 76.

12. Jung, *Collected Works*, vol. 8, para. 550.

13. Ibid., vol. 10, para. 441.

14. Robert Temple, *He Who Saw Everything: A Verse Translation of the Epic of Gilgamesh*.

15. Frank Cawson, "The Hero Must Die," manuscript in possession of the author.

16. Homer, *The Odyssey*, trans. Robert Fitzgerald. London: Collins Harvill, 1988.

17. Jung, *Memories, Dreams, Reflections*, p. 33.

Chapter 3: The Healing Wound

1. Jung, *Memories, Dreams, Reflections*, p. 109.

2. J. P. Henry and P. M. Stephens, *Stress, Health and the Social Environment: A Sociobiological Approach to Medicine*.

3. Stevens, *Archetypes.*

4. Fox, *Search for Society,* p. 215.

5. Ibid., p. 220.

6. John Bowlby, *Attachment and Loss,* vol. 1, *Attachment.*

7. Jung, *Collected Works,* vol. 16, para. 83, and vol. 7, para. 195.

8. The "father imago" is a term introduced by Jung to denote the complex image that develops in the psyche as a product of interaction between the personal father in the family environment and the father archetype in the collective unconscious.

9. Erik H. Erikson, *Identity and the Life Cycle.*

10. Bowlby, *Attachment and Loss,* vol. 2; W. R. D. Fairbairn, *Psychoanalytic Studies of the Personality;* D. W. Winnicott, *Playing and Reality.*

11. Bowlby, *Attachment and Loss,* vol. 2, pp. 109–10.

12. Price, "Alternative Channels for Negotiating Asymmetry."

13. M. R. A. Chance, Introduction to *Social Fabrics of the Mind,* ed. Chance, p. 3.

14. Anthony Storr, *The Dynamics of Creation,* p. 73.

15. George W. Brown and T. Harris, *Social Origins of Depression.*

16. Wenegrat, *Sociobiology and Mental Disorders,* p. 36; C. G. Jung, *The Integration of the Personality,* p. 8.

17. Jung, *Integration of the Personality,* p. 8. From childhood, Jung experienced himself as made up of two separate personalities, which he designated Number 1 and Number 2, respectively. Number 1 was his exact contemporary and enabled him to cope with the daily exigencies of life, while Number 2 was of infinite age, remote from the world of human society, but close to nature, animals, dreams, and God.

18. James Woodburn, "Egalitarian Societies," *Man* 17 (1982): 431–51.

19. Chance, *Social Fabrics of the Mind,* introduction, pp. 3–9.

20. Anthony F. C. Wallace, *Religion: An Anthropological View;* Anthony Stevens, *The Roots of War: A Jungian Perspective.*

21. Sigmund Freud, *Standard Edition,* vol. 23, *Analysis Terminable and Interminable,* p. 211.

22. Gordon Rattray Taylor, *Rethink.*

23. Gilbert, *Human Nature and Suffering*, p. 193.

24. Jung, *Collected Works*, vol. 10, para. 351.

25. Ibid., paras. 359, 361.

Chapter 4: The Therapeutic Quest

1. T. A. Lambo, "Further Neuropsychiatric Observations in Nigeria," *British Medical Journal* (1960): 1696–1704.

2. N. S. Kline, "Use of *Rauwolfia Serpentina* Benth. in Neuropsychiatric Conditions," *Annals of the New York Academy of Science* 59 (1954): 107–32; R. Prince, "The Use of Rauwolfia for the Treatment of Psychoses by Nigerian Native Doctors," *American Journal of Psychiatry* 117 (1960): 147–49.

3. P. P. Onyango, "The Views of African Mental Patients towards Mental Illness and Its Treatment," Master's thesis, University of Nairobi, 1976, quoted in Julian Leff, *Psychiatry around the Globe: A Transcultural View.*

4. Henri Ellenberger, *The Discovery of the Unconscious*, p. 38.

5. C. J. Groesbeck, "The Archetypal Image of the Wounded Healer," *Journal of Analytical Psychology* 20 (1975): 122–45.

6. D. H. Rosen, "Inborn Basis for the Healing Doctor-Patient Relationship," *Pharos* 55 (1992): 17–21.

7. Frederico Sal y Rosas, "El mito del Mani o Susto de la medicina indigena del Perú," *Revista Psiquiátrica Peruana* 1 (1957): 103–32.

8. N. J. Allen, "Approaches to Illness in the Nepalese Hills," in *Social Anthropology and Medicine*, ed. J. B. Loudon.

9. Leff, *Psychiatry around the Globe.*

10. Winnicott, *Playing and Reality*, p. 6.

11. M. J. Field, "Chronic Psychosis in Rural Ghana," *British Journal of Psychiatry* 114 (1968): pp. 31–33.

12. R. Prince, "Indigenous Yoruba Psychiatry," in *Magic, Faith and Healing*, ed. A. Kiev.

13. Alex Sakula, "In Search of Hippocrates: A Visit to Kos," *Journal of the Royal Society of Medicine* 77 (Aug., 1984): 682–88.

14. Alfred J. Ziegler, "Morbistic Rituals," in *The Meaning of Illness*, ed. Mark Kidel and Susan Rowe-Leete, pp. 155–70.

15. J. P. Henry, "Comment" (on *The Cerebral Hemispheres in Analytical Psychology* by Rossi). *Journal of Analytical Psychology* 22 (1977): 52–57.

16. Ziegler, "Morbistic Rituals," p. 162.

17. Ernest Rossi, "The Cerebral Hemispheres in Analytical Psychology," *Journal of Analytical Psychology* 22 (1977): 32–51.

18. Eugene Monick, *The Phallos: Sacred Image of the Masculine*.

19. K. M. Calestro, "Psychotheraphy, Faith Healing and Suggestions," *International Journal of Psychiatry* 10 (1972): R. Prince, "Variations in Psychotherapeutic Procedures," in *Handbook of Cross-Cultural Psychology*, vol. 6, *Psychopathology*.

20. R. Horton, "Destiny and the Unconscious in West Africa," *Africa* 31 (1961): 110–16.

EPILOGUE

1. Sigmund Freud, *The Interpretation of Dreams*, p. 148.

2. F. H. C. Crick and G. Mitchison, "The Function of Dream Sleep," *Nature* 304 (1983): 111–14; Freud, *Interpretation of Dreams*, pp. 149, 150 (Robert quoted on p. 149).

3. Liam Hudson, *Night Life: The Interpretation of Dreams*.

Bibliography

Allen, N. J. "Approaches to Illness in the Nepalese Hills." In *Social Anthropology and Medicine,* edited by J. B. Loudon, ASA Monograph No. 13. London: Academic Press, 1976.

Aserinsky, Eugene, and Nathaniel Kleitman. "Regularly Occurring Periods of Eye Motility and Concurrent Phenomena during Sleep." *Science* 118 (1953): 273–74.

Auden, W. H. *A Certain World.* London: Faber and Faber, 1971.

Bowlby, John. *Attachment and Loss.* Vol. 1, *Attachment;* and Vol. 2, *Separation: Anxiety and Anger.* London: Hogarth Press and the Institute of Psycho-Analysis, 1973.

Brown, George W., and T. Harris. *Social Origins of Depression.* London: Tavistock Publications, 1978.

Burson, Nancy. *Androgyne* (composite photograph). *Harper's,* June, 1985, p. 28.

Calestro, K. M. "Psychotherapy, Faith Healing and Suggestions." *International Journal of Psychiatry* 10 (1972): 83–113.

Chance, M. R. A., ed. *Social Fabrics of the Mind.* Hove and London: Lawrence Erlbaum Associates, 1988.

Chomsky, Noam. *Aspects of the Theory of Syntax.* Cambridge, Mass.: MIT Press, 1965.

Crick, F. H. C., and G. Mitchison. "The Function of Dream Sleep." *Nature* 304 (1983): 111–14.

D'Aquili, Eugene. "The Influence of Jung on the Works of Lévi-Strauss." *Journal of the History of Behavioural Science* 11 (1975).

Ellenberger, Henri. *The Discovery of the Unconscious.* New York: Basic Books, 1970.

Erikson, Erik H. *Identity and the Life Cycle.* Psychological Issues Monograph 1. New York: International Universities Press, 1959.

Evans, Christopher. *Landscapes of the Night: How and Why We Dream,* edited by Peter Evans. New York: Viking, 1983.

Fairbairn, W. R. D. *Psychoanalytic Studies of the Personality.* London: Tavistock Publications, 1952.

Field, M. J. "Chronic Psychosis in Rural Ghana." *British Journal of Psychiatry* 114 (1968): 31–33.

Fox, Robin. *Encounter with Anthropology,* London: Peregrine, 1975.

————. *The Search for Society.* New Brunswick, N.J.: Rutgers University Press, 1989.

Freud, Sigmund. *The Interpretation of Dreams.* London: Pelican Books, 1976.

————. *Standard Edition.* Vol. 23, *Analysis Terminable and Interminable.* London and New York: Hogarth Press and the Institute of Psycho-Analysis, 1937.

Gardner, Russell. "Psychiatric Syndromes as Infrastructure for Intraspecific Communication." In *Social Fabrics of the Mind,* edited by M. R. A. Chance. Hove and London: Lawrence Erlbaum Associates, 1988.

Gilbert, Paul. *Human Nature and Suffering.* Hove and London: Lawrence Erlbaum Associates, 1989.

Griffith, R. M., O. Miyagi, and A. Tago. "The Universality of Typical Dreams: Japanese versus Americans." *American Anthropologist* 60 (1958): 1173–78.

Groesbeck, C. J. "The Archetypal Image of the Wounded Healer," *Journal of Analytical Psychology* 20 (1975): 122–45.

Hall, Calvin S., and Vernon J. Norby. *The Individual and His Dreams.* New York: New American Library, 1972.

Henry, J. P. "Comment" (on *The Cerebral Hemispheres in Analytical Psychology* by Rossi). *Journal of Analytical Psychology* 22 (1977): 52–57.

————, and P. M. Stephens. *Stress, Health and the Social Environment:*

A Sociobiological Approach to Medicine. New York: Springer-Verlag, 1977.

Hillman, James. *The Dream and the Underworld.* New York: Harper & Row, 1979.

Hobson, J. Allan. *The Dreaming Brain.* New York: Basic Books, 1988.

Horton, R. "Destiny and the Unconscious in West Africa." *Africa* 31 (1961): 110–16.

Hudson, Liam. *Night Life: The Interpretation of Dreams,* London: Weidenfeld & Nicolson, 1985.

Jouvet, Michel. "The Function of Dreaming: A Neurophysiologist's Point of View." In *Handbook of Psychobiology,* edited by M. S. Gazzaniga and C. Blakemore. New York: Academic Press, 1975.

Jung, C. G. *The Collected Works of C. G. Jung,* edited by H. Read, M. Fordham, and G. Adler. London: Routledge and Kegan Paul, 1953–78; New York: Pantheon Books, 1953–60, and Bollingen Foundation, 1961–67; Princeton, N.J.: Princeton University Press, 1967–78.

————. *The Integration of the Personality.* London: Routledge & Kegan Paul, 1940.

————. *Memories, Dreams, Reflections,* recorded and edited by Aniela Jaffé. London: Collins and Routledge & Kegan Paul, 1963.

————. *Modern Man in Search of a Soul.* London: Kegan Paul, 1933.

————. *Psychological Reflections: A New Anthology of His Writings, 1905–1961,* selected and edited by Jolande Jacobi. London: Routledge & Kegan Paul, 1971.

————, and W. Pauli. *The Interpretation and Nature of the Psyche.* London: Routledge & Kegan Paul, 1955.

Kline, N. S. "Use of *Rauwolfia Serpentina* Benth. in Neuropsychiatric Conditions." *Annals of the New York Academy of Science* 59 (1954): 107–32.

Koepping, Klaus-Peter. *Adolf Bastian and the Psychic Unity of Mankind.* St. Lucia: University of Queensland Press, 1983.

Kugler, Paul. *The Alchemy of Discourse: An Archetypal Approach to Language.* Lewisberg, Pa.: Bucknell University Press, 1982.

Lambo, T. A. "Further Neuropsychiatric Observations in Nigeria." *British Medical Journal* (1960): 1696–1704.

Leff, Julian. *Psychiatry around the Globe: A Transcultural View.* London: Gaskell (The Royal College of Psychiatrists), 1981.

Lévi-Strauss, Claude. *The Savage Mind.* Chicago: University of Chicago Press, 1968.

———. *Structural Anthropology.* Garden City, N.Y.: Anchor, 1967.

Lumsden, Charles J., and Edward O. Wilson. *Promethean Fire: Reflections on the Origins of Mind.* Cambridge, Mass.: Harvard University Press, 1983.

MacLean, Paul D. *The Triune Concept of the Brain and Behaviour,* edited by T. J. Boag and D. Campbel. Toronto: University of Toronto Press, 1973.

Monick, Eugene. *The Phallos: Sacred Image of the Masculine.* Toronto: Inner City, 1987.

Morris, Desmond. *The Human Zoo.* London: Jonathan Cape, 1969.

Murdock, George P. "The Common Denominator of Culture." In *The Science of Man in the World Crisis,* edited by R. Linton. New York: Columbia University Press, 1945.

Price, John. "Alternative Channels for Negotiation Asymmetry in Social Relationships." In *Social Fabrics of the Mind,* edited by M. R. A. Chance, Hove and London: Lawrence Erlbaum Associates, 1988.

Prince, R., "Indigenous Yoruba Psychiatry." In *Magic, Faith and Healing,* edited by A. Kiev. London: Collier-Macmillan, 1964.

———. "The Use of Rauwolfia for the Treatment of Psychoses by Nigerian Native Doctors." *American Journal of Psychiatry* 117 (1960): 147–49.

———. "Variations in Psychotherapeutic Procedures." In *Handbook of Cross-Cultural Psychology.* Vol. 6, *Psychopathology,* edited by Harry C. Triandis and Juris G. Draguns. Boston: Allyn and Bacon, 1980.

Rosen, D. H. "Inborn Basis for the Healing Doctor-Patient Relationship," *Pharos* 55 (1992): 17–21.

Rossi, Ernest. "The Cerebral Hemispheres in Analytical Psychology." *Journal of Analytical Psychology* 22 (1977): 32–51.

Rycroft, Charles. *Anxiety and Neurosis*. Harmondsworth: Penguin Books, 1970.

Sagan, Carl. *The Dragons of Eden*. London: Hodder and Stoughton, 1977.

Sakula, Alex. "In Search of Hippocrates: A Visit to Kos." *Journal of the Royal Society of Medicine* 77 (August, 1984): 682–88.

Sal y Rosas, Frederico. "El mito del Mani o Susto de la medicina indigena del Perú," *Revista Psiquiátrica Peruana* 1 (1957): 103–32.

Stern, Paul J. *The Haunted Prophet*. New York: George Braziller, 1976.

Stevens, Anthony. *Archetypes: A Natural History of the Self*. New York: William Morrow & Co.: London: Routledge & Kegan Paul, 1982.

———. *The Roots of War: A Jungian Perspective*. New York: Paragon House, 1989.

———. *Withymead: A Jungian Community for the Healing Arts*. London: Coventure/Element Books, 1986.

Storr, Anthony. *The Dynamics of Creation*. London: Secker and Warburg, 1972.

Taylor, Gordon Rattray. *Rethink*. London: Secker-Warburg, 1972.

Temple, Robert. *He Who Saw Everything: A Verse Translation of the Epic of Gilgamesh*. London: Rides, 1991.

Tinbergen, Niko. *The Study of Instinct*. London: Oxford University Press, 1951.

Turner, Victor. "Body, Brain, and Culture." *Zygon* 18 (September, 1983): 221–45.

Waddington, C. H. *The Strategy of the Genes: A Discussion of Some Aspects of Theoretical Biology*. London: George Allen & Unwin, 1957.

Wallace, Anthony F. C. *Religion: An Anthropological View*. New York: Random House, 1966.

Wenegrat, Brant. *Sociobiology and Mental Disorder*, Menlo Park, Calif.: Addison-Wesley Publishing Company, 1984.

Winnicott, D. W. *Playing and Reality*. London: Tavistock Publications, 1971.

Woodburn, James. "Egalitarian Societies." *Man* 17 (1982): 431–51.

Ziegler, Alfred J. "Morbistic Rituals." In *The Meaning of Illness*, edited by Mark Kidel and Susan Rowe-Leete. London: Routledge, 1988.

Index